MW00648471

it's
temporary,
babe!

Copyright @ 2023 Cassandra DeCicco
It's Temporary, Babe! From Heartbreak to Happiness and Finding It Within Myself.

YGTMedia Co. Trade Paperback Edition.
ISBN trade paperback: 978-1-998754-12-0
eBook: 9978-1-998754-13-7
All Rights Reserved. No part of this book can be scanned, distributed, or copied without permission. This book or any portion thereof may not be reproduced or used in any manner whatsoever without the express written permission of the publisher at publishing@ygtmedia.co—except for the use of brief quotations in a book review.

The author has made every effort to ensure the accuracy of the information within this book was correct at time of publication. Some names have been changed to protect the identity of those discussed. The author does not assume and hereby disclaims any liability to any party for any loss, damage, or disruption caused by errors or omissions, whether such errors or omissions result from accident, negligence, or any other cause. This book is not intended to be a substitute for the medical advice of a licensed physician. The reader should consult with their doctor in any matters relating to their health.

The publisher is not responsible for websites (or their content) that are not owned by the publisher.

Published in Canada, for Global Distribution by YGTMedia Co.
www.ygtmedia.co/publishing
To order additional copies of this book: publishing@ygtmedia.co
Edited by Kelly Lamb
Interior design and typesetting by Doris Chung
Cover design by Michelle Fairbanks
Author Photo by Alexa Fiskaa

TORONTO

FROM **HEARTBREAK**
TO HAPPINESS AND FINDING
IT WITHIN MYSELF

it's temporary, babe!

CASSANDRA
DECICCO

This book is dedicated to Nanny, my guardian angel.
Thank you for sending me the message to write this
book and share my story.
I love and miss you every day.

table of contents

introduction

There I was, in the bathroom line of a very crowded bar, when I noticed a girl in front of me, puffy faced, with tears rolling out of her eyes, clearly crying to herself.

"Are you okay?" I asked.

"No, I'm not," she said, in her slightly tipsy but emotional state.

What is it about girls and bar bathrooms that make you feel like everyone you meet is your best friend who you need to tell your whole life story to?

"My fiancé and I just broke up. I think . . . I don't know. He wants space out of nowhere and he wouldn't tell me why and we just bought a house and a girl I don't know started following him on Instagram last night!" She was half slurring and half crying.

"Ugh, screw him!" I replied. "If he doesn't see how great you are, then that's his loss. C'mon, let me buy you a drink!" I offered, trying to pep her up. What I really wanted to say to her was, *Geez, Girl—you have NO idea the emotional roller coaster that is coming for you. You are only in the very beginning, and the worst is definitely not over.*

Of course, I couldn't say that to her—this poor, broken, fragile girl. I had been in her shoes not too long ago, and if someone had said that to me, it would have destroyed me. Unfortunately, it was the truth. Maybe a warning would have been easier? I don't know. On the other hand, I also would have told her that these feelings she was having—the pain, sadness, and confusion—would pass, eventually. It would get better, and she would come out stronger and more secure than ever. *And how this could be the best thing to ever happen to her in the end.*

The number of people I have come across over the years who have gone through this same scenario, or a similar situation, is higher than I can count. I would say to myself all of the time, "I'm going to write a book one day. I'm going to be there for women who have experienced heartbreak similar to mine feel like they aren't alone. I'm going to give them hope that not only will they feel normal again, but they will be happier than ever and that it is all, *eventually*, going to be okay."

How do I know this? A month after my magical wedding day, my then husband said the very same thing to me. It was over before it even started—but it didn't end there.

Grab your favorite notebook for when you are reading along, as each chapter offers journal prompts for you to explore and document your own journey!

my "fairy tale"

Once upon a time, on an island somewhere in between New Jersey and Brooklyn, there was a girl who was minding her own damn business, going to high school, and working at a bakery in the middle of town. She fell in love with the funny guy of the friend group, got married ten years later, only to be betrayed less than thirty days after their I dos. With her heart completely broken, she drank her feelings away, swiped for hours on dating apps, and hit rock bottom. But this wouldn't be the end of her story. She would not stay in this state forever. She found a courage she never knew she had, started going to therapy, and found her authentic self and worth during the process.

Okay, so this is definitely not a fairy tale, but it is a

pretty incredible story, if I do say so myself. Let's start at the beginning. My name is Cassandra DeCicco and I am thirty-something years old. I grew up in Staten Island, New York, with my mom, dad, older sister, older brother, and twin sister, Emma. Emma and I are total opposites but have always been best friends and each other's other half in life—then and now. When I was growing up, my house always had an open door, and friends, family, and neighbors were in and out constantly. There was a lot of love, a lot of laughs, a lot of food, and *a lot* of mixed personalities. It's no surprise that our childhoods shape us into who we are as adults, but it wasn't until my WTF moment when I realized how true this was. Growing up in this environment, I became an empath and a people pleaser who was always scared to be alone. I am a little bit of a neat freak, a homebody, and someone who loves hosting and having a lot of people around. We lived paycheck to paycheck, but we never knew it. Our house was filled with love and 5 p.m. family dinners every day mixed with arguments and yelling once a week when my parents sat down at the table to do the bills. With a strong dislike for conflict, I would shut down at the first sight of it. I became so used to the inconsistency in my household that it felt normal to me, and I didn't know how to communicate or express my emotions for most of my life. Despite this, there was nothing I loved more than being around my family.

As a kid, I always pictured myself married, in a big house, taking care of my husband, and having kids running around everywhere. I met my high school sweetheart, Tony, at sixteen, and we were married by twenty-six. We grew up together, and even though we were young, we were very much in love. I remember feeling happier than ever when we married. Sadly, only one month later, my world was turned upside down. Tony, the love of my young adulthood, left me for a 21-year-old girl he had just met at the gym a few weeks before. I was crushed, blindsided, and absolutely devastated. I was losing my best friend and my partner of over ten years, and there was nothing I could do about it.

I had very low self-worth to begin with, and I couldn't imagine ever bouncing back from the hole I was in. I lost my person, my house, my extended family, my group of friends, and I was living by myself for the first time in my entire life. I started doing anything and everything to numb the pain that I was feeling. Instead of dealing with the pain, I buried everything, hoping it all would just disappear. I worked ten-hour days and spent all of my free time excessively drinking and swiping on dating apps looking for my worth in all the wrong places. I was in a dark place and found myself at a crossroad. I could keep going down the destructive path I was on or learn from my experience and try to become a better person, which is exactly what I did.

How though? How do you take a shattered life and build something incredible from it? There were a few things that became my lifeline during those dark years. I found peace in journaling every step of the way, and I explored my spirituality and was committed to lean into my faith for the first time in my life. I focused on positivity and acceptance while really working on self-awareness and creating a life that I was in love with—*on my own.* I focused on where I wanted to be instead of what happened to me in the past. I became devoted to going inward and healing the things I had been pushing away from before my relationship and strived to be a version of myself that I liked. I became someone I would choose, someone I trusted.

LET'S CHECK IN

So often, we think, "Why am I like this?"

Going back and starting with how we grew up is a great first step to bring awareness to certain patterns. Think about your childhood and describe it in one sentence.

moving forward, sort of

Tony and I had met when I was sixteen and he was eighteen. We were such babies! He was a six-two Italian American from Staten Island. He had a stocky build with thick, dark brown hair, and dark brown eyes. When he wasn't wearing jeans and clunky work boots, he sported a black t-shirt, sweatpants, and a new pair of Nikes. He had a very loud truck, was always the center of attention, and was the ultimate jokester of the group. I had never met someone who could make me laugh so effortlessly the way he did. He was very confident and silly at the same time. The first night we met, we clicked immediately. I felt connected to him right off the bat, even though it wasn't in a romantic way. He was reliable, caring, and gave the best bear hugs. He had such a sense of safety about him, something I wasn't used to in my life. His strong work ethic was admirable. If we were driving somewhere and he saw someone stuck on the side of the road, he would always pull over and offer to help them.

Tony and I were friends for about six months before we started dating. The first few months of our relationship, he made me feel like the luckiest girl in the entire world. I felt so appreciated and special for the *first time* in my life. He cared about my feelings and would do absolutely anything for me. He insisted on driving me to and picking me up from work and school (I didn't even have my license yet!). He was respectful and accepted my family despite any craziness that went on. He would surprise me with thoughtful gifts like when he once bought me one hundred packs of my favorite gum, and he treated Emma, my twin, as if she was his little sister. He would spend hours decorating my house with Christmas lights, so my dad didn't have to do it. He even had our names made into a decal and plastered it on the back of his truck. Everyone knew how in love we were, and I felt so grateful to have met my match so early in life. We were together for four years, which in teen years felt like a lifetime, before the relationship became stagnant and we decided to take a break from one another. Our dynamic started to shift, and the excitement we had in the beginning started to fizzle out. We were so close and so comfortable (even though we were still so young) and almost ready to take those next steps like moving in together and getting engaged. He was my first real boyfriend, my first serious relationship, and the first and only person I'd had sex with. During this time, we started to feel bored with one another, which led to fighting over the smallest things, causing us to question our relationship. At that crossroad, we mutually agreed to take some time apart and figure ourselves out.

We both dated other people, and after being apart for almost a year, we found ourselves right back together and more confident in our relationship. Still, we were only twenty-two and twenty-four, respectively. However, we chose to grow together while also giving each other the space we needed as individuals. We decided to move in together in an apartment on the side of his childhood home, on Staten Island, and focused on growing our careers. I had graduated from Fashion School in Manhattan and was working in the Garment Center. Tony had worked for the union repairing and installing heating and air conditioning units in all of the buildings in New York City. We were both low maintenance, mostly homebodies, and not huge into the club or bar scene like a lot of our friends were. We worked really hard for anything we wanted in life, and our focus was to save money. We spent our nights on the couch eating ice cream and watching *The Sopranos* with our dog, Jessica. Living together for the first time brought us even closer. We were falling asleep together every night and waking up next to another every morning. They say moving in either makes a couple or breaks them—and for us, it definitely made us.

When it came to family, values, and work ethic, we were so similar. We had a solid foundation between us. However, there were some significant differences. Tony was a workaholic. He never said no to a job or to making extra money. I would be ready to pass out by 9 p.m., which did not align with him working all day and his 11 p.m. dinners.

If you are not familiar with love languages, there is a book called *The Five Love Languages* by Gary Chapman that I recommend to everyone I meet. This book is so simple yet makes a lot of sense when it comes to couples, or any type of relationship for that matter, and how they show love in relationships. Tony's love language was definitely Acts of Service (showing love with actions, instead of words, i.e., working, paying the bills, fixing your car). This was the way he showed love and received it. I wish I had known more about love languages back then!

My love language is Quality Time (undivided attention and spending time together) and Physical Touch (holding hands, hugs, kisses, a pat on the bum). It was in these areas where we didn't mix. I have vivid memories of trying to hold his hand in the car or while walking. He would fling his hand away because it irked him so much, and in return, I would feel like I wanted to cry on the spot. While we had our life together, the balance of time alone versus time together was definitely off. We both gave each other the space to let each other do the things that made us happy. I loved Tony and figured he worked so hard, he should be able to spend his free time doing what he wanted. Why should I make him come away with my family and me for a weekend if that's not what he wanted to do? I still had that peacemaker role I took on as a child and would keep quiet to avoid conflict. He never held me back from going out to dinners or taking a trip to California to see my best friend for a week. I remember going abroad for college for two weeks to Italy and Spain, and the boyfriend of one of the girls I was traveling with was constantly calling her. He was fighting with her for not keeping in touch and accusing her of not being truthful to him. I felt so lucky and relieved that Tony was not like that. We never really fought. We would bicker about silly things, but that was the extent of it. We trusted each other completely and respected each other, but in some ways, we almost gave one another too much space. Eventually, this became an issue for us. Some nights, I went to the car shop and stood there freezing while he worked on his truck just to spend time with him, but I was completely miserable. There were times when we would get dressed up and go out to eat somewhere I wanted, but he would be tired and cranky the whole time from working all day. He hated going out in general.

I found myself constantly making excuses for him as to why he didn't attend certain social gatherings or why we couldn't go out when we were always invited. If we had plans one night, I would spend the entire day walking on eggshells as I spoke to him, trying to grasp the chance of him showing up or not, and I would never get a straight answer. I never knew if I was going to go out alone up until ten minutes before leaving. Most times, I would end up going by myself, even with his friends and family. He never planned dates or exciting things for us to do; I would always do it. And it was like pulling teeth for us to get us there. It would make me sad because I genuinely liked being around him and felt he made everything more fun. We were best friends and partners in life, but we lacked the chemistry and excitement you would normally see in a relationship of two people in their twenties. We were already stuck in a routine, the cycle of working all day, having dinner, watching a show, and passing out. Once the weekend came, we would do our own thing. This was our life, on repeat. We didn't go on cute dates or have those moments where we couldn't keep our hands off each other. I resigned myself to thinking that we'd been together for seven years and that's just what happens. When I look back now, I could shake myself—the version of me that was so insecure and enmeshed in the relationship, convincing herself that Tony's needs, wants, and interests were more important than hers.

I reflect back and realize that as much as he did love me and accept me, I always wanted to feel like he *genuinely* liked me, which looking back, I rarely felt. In relationships, at what point do you acknowledge and accept each other's differences and compromise versus totally going against who you are and what you like to do?

LET'S CHECK IN

As I mentioned, I didn't know about love languages then. I just thought love was easy, and it didn't require more than just feeling that emotion. Maybe you've thought this or something similar too.

- How do you feel loved in a relationship?
- How do you feel you show love to others?

Feel free to write as much or as little as you like. If you've never thought about love like this, I think it will help in creating a clearer understanding of what love is to you.

intuition

Unlike a lot of our other friends who were also in relationships, we often spoke about what we wanted in life like getting married, buying a house, and having kids. But I wasn't obsessed with the idea of getting engaged and married right away. Some of the girls in our circle would talk about it like it was the finish line or something, and I didn't get it. Yes, I wanted to get engaged to Tony, but deep down, something about it felt off. I now realize it was me wanting to feel that he really wanted to be with me. He would constantly tell me how much he loved me, that I was his rock in life, and that he would be lost without me; however, everything and everyone else were prioritized before me, and his actions didn't match up with his words. I clung to these words, though. That is what we do, right?! Cling to the positive and ignore the negatives because it just feels so much better this way. Again, this was a pattern and the norm in my house growing up, and I continued accepting it into my adult life.

As time went on, we decided we wanted to be responsible and buy a house together before getting engaged. We had lived together and knew it was what we wanted, and instead of spending our money on rings and a wedding, while not having a place of our own, we started house hunting. We ended up purchasing a townhouse together in 2014, a few towns over from where we were living. It was the beginning of this new, adult chapter of our lives. I was so proud of how far we had come, and we could not have been happier. Trips to Home Depot, doing house projects, and barbequing with our friends and family became our new favorite things to do. Tony left the decorating to me, and I had the house painted in different shades of grays. We found a similar style when decorating, which was exciting since our first apartment was pretty much a merge of both of our childhood bedrooms. We were spending more quality time together than ever before, and I was so thrilled. We hosted our first Thanksgiving that year with both of our families combined. It felt amazing to replicate the happy times that I had growing up. We were already making so many great memories in this house.

Tony and I were in our new house for about six months. It was February 24, 2015, and I had just returned home from a cold, long day in NYC. I always felt lucky to live so close to Manhattan. So many people uproot their whole lives to experience the city, and some never get the chance to at all. While I always wanted to take advantage of the opportunities it had to offer (I went to college uptown and worked in midtown), I didn't necessarily love the city, to be honest. Even when I lived in the college dorm for a year, I came home any chance I could to have one of Dad's home-cooked meals. At the end of the day, Manhattan completely and absolutely drained me. I felt like my days were constantly filled with battling the unpredictable East Coast weather and racing among a herd of cattle during rush hour to and from the office. I would feel so much lighter the second I stepped off the bus in Staten Island to head home at the end of the day.

When I arrived home, all of the lights were off, which was weird because Tony was always home before me, and he didn't tell me that he was working late. I called him to see what he wanted for dinner.

He said he was with his brother Matt, and that they had to fix something at Tina's, Matt's girlfriend at the time. *That's weird*, I thought. I was talking to Tina that day and she didn't say anything about Tony going over there. *It must have just broken.* Tina and I had become so close. Matt lived next door to us, and Tina and I would spend countless hours on the weekends at my kitchen table drinking coffee and talking about anything and everything. Matt, Tina, and I would usually go to dinner or watch movies together when Tony was working. They would often include me in everything.

I walked upstairs and started looking for the biggest most comfortable sweatpants I could find to get rid of the chill I still had from the freezing city that day. I threw my hair in a ponytail and washed my makeup off. I remember thinking how pale I looked since it was the middle of February, and I was desperately lacking some Vitamin D. I also remember getting a strong whiff of Tony's cologne as I was getting undressed. He would only wear cologne if he went out, and if he had put it on in the morning, the smell would have been long gone by the time he had arrived home. *Weird.*

I heard the door open with a loud, "Helllooo!"

It was our thing; the way we always greeted each other. "Helllooo! I'm up here," I responded. A few minutes went by, and he met me in our bedroom. He gave me a big hug and kiss and asked me about my day.

"Why are you wearing cologne?"

"I put it on before I went to Tina's. I am filthy from work and didn't want to go to her house smelling bad."

We both laughed as I kissed him all over his face, shoving my nose in his neck, smelling the cologne I loved so much. I believed him. I didn't think he was being shady or anything, but something inside of me thought, *I feel like he's not telling me the truth*. I was so quick to push my intuition down and not trust myself. We walked downstairs, and he stopped by the front door as I walked into the kitchen.

"Can you check if my keys are in the bowl? I left my charger in the car and don't want to walk over there with my boots on."

The "bowl" was a big pedestal mercury decorative bowl that we had on the server in the dining room. I am kind of a neat freak and had bought it to put things that were lying around the house so Tony would always know where to find them. He loved leaving keys, chargers, change, his wallet *everywhere*, and it drove me bonkers! So this became a universal place of all "lost things."

I walked over to the bowl, and there was a big red box in it. As much as I clearly knew at that moment what was going on, I had no idea what was going on! A hope was filled at that moment when Tony proposed right there in our living room. I didn't question my response for a second and said a wholehearted, "Yes!"

It was the happiest moment of my entire life. The ring was beautiful. It was his grandmother's stone that he'd had reset; it was so sentimental and perfect. Matt came barging in giving us the biggest hugs and asking, "Did you know?"

"I had absolutely no idea!" *Besides him wearing cologne at 7 p.m.*, I thought. I was so surprised. Our families and friends came over that night, and as we started taking pictures that flooded our Facebook and Instagram feeds, I said to myself, *Case, you definitely need a tan! And why did you put on your biggest pair of sweatpants tonight of ALL nights?* Despite this, I was so happy I could have filled the whole world with my joy that night.

LET'S CHECK IN

That's the funny thing about our intuition, we automatically think, "Oh, it's nothing" or "I'm being paranoid." *Why would someone I love lie?* Meanwhile, deep down, you know you're right. Something was off and even though it was for an amazing surprise, I still sensed this energy inside me and chose to completely ignore it.

I don't know why you're here, and I don't know what you may be going through at this moment, but I do know that writing it out helps. As often as possible, write out the answers to these questions. When you do, not only will you discover something about yourself that will help with your situation, but you will also learn something that will strengthen your relationship with yourself.

- Reflect on a time when your intuition was speaking to you.
- Where were you feeling it? Head? Stomach? Chest?
- Did you ignore it or trust it?
- Was it ultimately right?

insecurity

As I stood there in the thirty-fifth wedding dress I had tried on, staring at myself in the mirror and looking around the room at my family and friends' bright faces, all waiting for some type of reaction from me, I finally said, "I don't *hate* it."

Everyone talks about that moment when you try on your wedding dress and how you'll just "know." In *Say Yes to the Dress*, there are moments when everyone starts crying as soon as the bride walks out because she found the "perfect one." Well, I never even got close to any of that. I actually think that type of experience is not what the majority of brides feel. Then they feel bad and insecure when it doesn't happen. That was my experience, at least.

I could tell everyone was getting fed up with me—I was getting fed up with myself. I was overwhelmed by insecurities and doubt and mainly thinking, *I don't think he is going to like this one.* I finally said it out loud, but twisted it a little. "I just really want something that he is going to like; it's his day too."

Looking back, I can see they all saw how pathetic and insecure I sounded. Tina and Emma were also engaged at this point, and I remember thinking, *Why do their experiences with wedding dress shopping feel so different from mine?*

My future mother-in-law blurted out, "Who cares what he thinks?!"

She loved me as if I were her own daughter, and many people thought we were blood-related. I brushed her off with my usual, "You're so mean to him." The truth was, I was painfully insecure in general. I never thought much of myself and my appearance. I had been dieting on and off for as long as I could remember, and having everyone stare at me in a big white dress was just bringing a lot of those body image issues out. Growing up, I was always labeled as the "bigger twin." I was eight pounds when we were born, and Emma was four pounds. I was literally the size of two of her! She was tall, slender, with dark curly hair and always looked so naturally beautiful. I would cry to my mom all of the time about my big butt and boobs that had developed before any of my friends. She would listen and tell me that I was beautiful, but she would add that I was "big boned" and "voluptuous," which no 15-year-old would take as a good thing! I definitely suffered from body dysmorphia, but I now see that I really just was an average and healthy teenager. Along with those insecurities, when it came to my relationship with Tony, I never felt enough for him. He consistently criticized the way I dressed, suggesting I should wear tighter clothes even though I felt uncomfortable in them. The thought of him being disappointed in the way I looked on our wedding day absolutely consumed me. I stayed up at night obsessing and thinking about it even after I had chosen a dress.

I constantly second-guessed myself and would drop passive-aggressive hints and questions to him to gauge if the dress I picked would be something he would like. I would pull up a picture on Instagram of someone we knew who just got married and say, "Wow, she looks beautiful. What do you think?"

And if he responded with any criticism—"She does, but it should be more of x, y, and z"—I would panic, picking my dress apart to see if it aligned with what he was saying. Pathetic, I know. Many may wonder why I was marrying someone who made me feel like this. The truth was, it really wasn't him making me feel this way; it was the internal dialogue I'd had within myself long before I even met him that always said, *You are just not good enough.* For whatever reason, I felt like I didn't deserve all of the good happening in my life. I felt like I wasn't good enough to have the guy, the wedding, and the house. I was surrounded by the nagging fear of judgment from people around me.

My insecurities became heightened in my relationship with him. I was always seeking validation from him to heal so much of my own trauma I had never dealt with. Sure, Tony's constant judgment and criticism and always wanting a bigger and better in life in general didn't help the situation, but really, it was all me and my inability to take a step back and acknowledge what I wanted or how I wanted to feel. I didn't even know what I wanted or what I liked because I was solely focused on making him happy first. I wanted him to feel that he was lucky to have me. When I look back, I see I had a big void within myself that I was trying to fill through him, by me wanting to feel loved and special. I was an empath and a people pleaser with no self-worth, who was completely in love with a man who did love me but was judgmental. I didn't see this when I was in the relationship, but we never do, right?! It was a recipe for disaster, and I don't even blame him because I enabled him. It became an ongoing dynamic of me keeping my feelings and needs quiet, then lashing out at little things that didn't really matter. He would make me the center of all his jokes, but then he'd follow it along with a big hug and kiss and tell me how much he loved me, that I was the best thing in his life. Again, I clung to those words far more than those actions.

Having Tony by my side and happy validated me as a person, even though I didn't even respect who that person was deep down. Tony was strong and admired; he was a real man in my eyes. Despite his faults, I knew I could count on him for anything I ever needed or wanted when it came down to it. We always had each other's backs, and he made me feel safe and secure. This is the problem, though, when you put all of your worth and value onto another person, especially at such a young age. I know now that it is not their job to complete you or to fill you up. I was setting myself up for disappointment. I realize this was a pattern in my relationship and my marriage. I was so used to saying yes to things I really wanted to say no to, and before I knew it I was living a life I was not comfortable or secure in, causing me to be a shell of myself I did not recognize.

LET'S CHECK IN

It wasn't until I was on my own and on my own self-worth journey that I realized my sense of confidence came from within myself. I went inward and paid attention to the times I felt the most insecure, and they were the times that I wasn't being truly authentic and true to myself. The more I drifted from my own values and what I was comfortable with, the more insecure I became. The more I ignored my voice inside of me telling me that something didn't feel right, the more detached I became from my true self. No matter how many diets I went on or how many gyms I joined, I was never going to feel confident and secure on the outside, because I wasn't on the inside.

I stopped trying to be someone that I wasn't and stopped trying to fit the mold of the people around me. I stopped being the people pleaser and the "yes, no problem" girl. I stopped worrying about or changing my look for a specific guy I was dating or jump on the crop top trend when that's what everyone around me was wearing.

I started paying attention to how I was feeling inside and worked toward being my true and authentic self. I dressed in what I was truly comfortable in for my body and became more confident than ever.

- Reflect on the last time you felt your absolute best. What were you wearing?
- What were you doing?
- Who were you with?
- How can you incorporate this confidence more into your daily routine?

this can't be happening

The year of 2016 was filled with wedding planning, renovating our new house that we had bought after getting engaged, and being a part of all of our friends' and siblings' wedding events. It was like we were all on the same timeline, and it felt right. It also felt like we were "on track" and doing what we were "supposed to be doing." On December 2, 2016, we had the most perfect wedding day. It truly was the best day of my entire life. It resembled a big fat Italian wedding, and I wouldn't have done it any other way. I had such a sense of relief and calm the whole day. From the minute I woke up, I felt immense happiness and could not wait to see my future husband and exchange our vows. I practiced them in the mirror probably fifty times and still managed to mess them up.

Tony had slept at his mother's house the night before, and it was so weird sleeping in our bed without him. We had rarely slept apart since moving in together. We decided to do a first look so we could take our pictures and enjoy the day. Tony was shaking, just like he was the night he proposed, except this time, we were in front of all our friends and families. He started sobbing when he saw me and hugged me tighter than he'd ever hugged me before. The feeling and that moment were who we really were in the midst of all the craziness that was going on in our lives that past year, and it all felt so right. There was so much love in the room, and for the first time ever, it was like he had placed me on a pedestal the whole night. He couldn't stop looking at me, hugging me, kissing me, and picking up my dress (that he did end up loving) when I needed it. There was not one sarcastic dig the whole night—it really does not take much to make me happy—and I felt beyond special. I thought, *Wow, if this is what being married to him is going to be like, I cannot wait!* We left two days later for our honeymoon in Mexico, and it was just as beautiful. It was the most quality time we had spent together all year. I couldn't imagine ever coming down from that high. We were so connected, and it seemed like we were finally on the same page.

We arrived back from our honeymoon in the middle

of December. It was so nice to be back home in our new house, which was fully decorated for Christmas. We had gone from Thanksgiving to our wedding to Mexico and right into my favorite season, Christmas. Tony was not happy to be back from Mexico at all. He loved being away and was cranky the very next day that we had to get back to work and back into our real-life routines. I didn't blame him, though. It was a lot to come down from. We had gone from a hot and sunny ninety-degree bliss to freezing weather and a snowstorm, scrambling to get ready for Christmas. To cheer him up, I went and bought everything to make the special breakfast he had ordered every morning on our honeymoon: ham and goat cheese on an English muffin. It was much better at the resort, but it was the thought that counted. We spent the holidays with our families and couldn't have ended the year on a better note. I felt at peace to have the wedding planning, the move, and the renovations of our new house behind us and was ready to start our life as a married couple after all of this time.

After Christmas, the entire energy in the house shifted. Something inside of me was alerting me that something was wrong, very wrong. You know the day after your birthday or Christmas when you just kind of feel sad? That "it's all done" feeling after being so happy? Well, we had that times one thousand. Thanksgiving, our wedding, the honeymoon, and Christmas had been the highlight reel, and now, we were in that dark, gray, weird week in between Christmas and New Year's.

At the time, I thought this was the shift that I had picked up on. Tony was super distant, and I chalked it up to him being depressed from having all of these exciting things going on to having nothing to look forward to. I knew what he was feeling. I always get sad taking down my Christmas decorations. As usual, Tony went right back into work mode, but I was off that whole week from work. I really missed not being with him! I also hated that he was clearly in such a bad mood, and that I felt this strong disconnect between us. Regardless of the ups and downs of our relationship, he'd never shut me out. I felt it in my bones that something was wrong—and I was right. On New Year's Day, he sat me down and told me that he wasn't in love with me and that he didn't want to be with me anymore.

I just stood there, frozen, while my brain tried to process the words that were coming out of his mouth. Of course, we weren't perfect, but this was the last thing I thought he was going to say. I didn't know where any of this was coming from. I truly didn't believe a word he was saying. I swear, I almost thought he was kidding. I may have even let out a little laugh when I think back to it. We were at the height of our relationship, we hadn't been this great in a long time, at least that's what I thought. I didn't make him get married; I didn't pressure him into this life. If anything, he was leading our life the way he wanted, and I was just in the passenger seat of his pickup truck along for the ride.

There was no talking him out of it, and I was completely devastated. I asked him if there was someone else, which he immediately denied. None of it made sense. I was sitting there talking to someone I didn't know anymore. He was not Tony. His eyes were blank and empty as he repeated, "I don't love you."

He was not my husband, not the man I had spent the last eleven years with, not the man I had recently said "I do" to in front of 260 people. I felt gut-punched, and I had nowhere to turn. The roof felt as if it was about to fall on top of me. I couldn't call even Emma about it; how could I explain this to anyone? None of it made sense, and I couldn't bear to say any of it out loud. We sat in silence for a while, and I swallowed my tears, trying to process the things I had just heard. I begged him to go to therapy, but he declined. It was over, and there was nothing I could do to change his mind.

The shift between us was something I could have never imagined. He acted as if I didn't exist. He left before I woke up, barely looked or spoke to me when he saw me, stopped texting me, and would come home after I was asleep. It was the emptiest and loneliest I have ever felt, still sleeping right next to the person who I loved more than anything, who was also my best friend. I started drinking bottles of wine every night to help me fall asleep. I was shocked, and embarrassed. I didn't feel comfortable talking to anyone about what had happened, not even my twin sister who I told *everything* to.

Going through this experience, as much as it shocked and destroyed me, forced me to go inward and take care of myself. I was always running around, being there for everyone else, and worrying about others, and at this point, I needed to be that person for me. I had to be *kind* to myself. I had to be strong because I couldn't let this take me down. There were a lot of highs and lows, and I didn't always choose the right coping mechanisms, but I did show myself compassion and grace through them. While I am in no way saying anyone should go through anything alone because there are so many amazing resources out there, the way you want to get through a tough time will start with you.

LET'S CHECK IN

Have you ever felt so low you never thought you would feel better again?

- How did you cope with these feelings?
- What did you do?
- Did you find yourself masking feelings of hurt or were you able to self-soothe through them in a healthy way?

I encourage you to make a list of things you do during a tough time and reflect which ones help you heal versus which ones keep you stuck.

divorce

Anytime I felt hurt in the past, Tony was who I went to, and he made it all better with a joke and a big hug. Now, he was the reason for the hurting, and I had nowhere to turn. I knew how ridiculous this whole thing sounded, and the thought of saying out loud what was just said to me seemed impossible. I replayed the past week, the past month, the past year over and over throughout the days and nights. I stopped sleeping. I couldn't eat. My body had a physical reaction to what was going on. I couldn't pinpoint the one thing that triggered this for him. I kept blaming myself, wondering what I did wrong. What did I say? What did I do to make him feel like this suddenly?

I had continued going to work preparing for a big trip

to London, and I had to leave in a few days. I blocked out what was going on in my personal life while I was at work, then I would cry the whole way home.

I was on the phone with Emma on my way home from work, still not telling her anything that was going on because I hadn't accepted any of it yet, and I ended up saying, "Why don't you meet me in London?!"

She laughed. "I'm getting married in two months. I don't know if I could pull it off, but OMG, I would love that."

"Aw, I know," I responded. "I have two free days, and you've always wanted to go. My room is paid for, and I'll pay for everything else if you can just get the flight. When will we ever get the chance to do this again?"

I was trying to amp it up for her to want to come on a fun trip with me, but really the idea of going to London in this emotional state and having two days by myself seemed like something I wouldn't have been able to go through alone.

Emma responded, "I know, you're probably going to be pregnant before we know it."

Little did she know. I had such a pit in my stomach hearing this from her. It was no secret that Tony and I wanted kids, and this was one of the many losses of the life I had planned, realizing it was no longer there.

I don't know if it was a twin thing or what, but the next

day, Emma called me and said, "I booked a flight. I'm meeting you in London!"

Tears of relief instantly started tumbling down my face. Emma was my best friend in the whole world, my other half, and at this time when I felt so alone and lost, she was going to be with me. After the relief of her coming settled in, I thought, *Yikes, I don't know how I am going to spend all this time with her without her knowing something is up.* I didn't want to tell her because I did not accept that this was really going on. Also, she was getting married in a few months to an amazing guy, Dom, and I didn't want to give her anything to worry about when it came to married life. I still had that caretaker role, especially when it came to her. *I'll figure it out*, I thought.

I remember sitting on the big velvet couch in the hotel lobby and the smell of the vanilla Earl Grey tea I was drinking when I saw Emma enter the lobby of the hotel. We ran up and hugged each other as if we hadn't seen each other in years. We always greeted each other like this even if we were together the day before, but this was an extra special happy dance hugging moment! We checked in and bundled up in our hats and scarves and spent the day sightseeing. It was a cold and rainy January day in London. We took one of the big red buses that hit every stop: Big Ben, Tower of London Bridge, Buckingham Palace—we didn't skip anything! The cold was something we were used to in New York, but the constant crisp air caught up to us, and we bought the most delicious hot chocolate right outside Westminster Abbey as we walked around the historic streets. With our bodies completely frozen, we ended the day at a little pub on a small cobblestoned side street where we ordered fish and chips and macaroons for dessert. At one point she said, "You look really pretty. Let me take your picture."

Really? Pretty? I was so jet-lagged. I knew I had bags under my eyes from crying for six days straight. And I was bundled up in my big turtleneck with hat hair, but I agreed.

"You okay?" She asked after she took the picture. I looked out the window watching people as they walked by and started to tear up. "No, I'm not."

"Everything will be okay," she responded. I knew she picked up on my energy that something wasn't right. I nodded, and we went back to our hotel. We passed out right away in what felt like the most comfortable bed ever after the long day we had.

The rest of the trip was a blur. Emma had friends she met up with while I worked, and we made the most of our time there. Everyone at work wanted to see my wedding rings and pictures of the reception while asking questions about every single detail, since they were based in the London office. I should have gotten an Academy Award for that performance having to relive it all. But I had to separate my grief. I had to for my mental health, especially if I was going to successfully kill it at the meetings that were taking place, which I did.

These limbo moments, when you don't know what to do or how to feel, and you just keep going through the motions, were my current coping mechanism. The only thing I did know, for whatever reason, was that I had to go to St. Paul's Cathedral where Princess Diana got married. We kept missing the hours to go, and I don't know why, but I felt compelled to visit there. I was determined to go before we left. Emma and I woke up early on our last day to go visit before heading to the airport. We arrived as soon as they opened the doors and went our separate ways once inside. I have been to many churches in my life, but I felt a weight lift off me once I walked into this one. Staring up at the huge ceilings and looking around, I started to feel very connected, light, and emotional. I am not very religious; I was brought up Catholic and would mostly go to church with my Nanny on Christmas Eve. It was always to make her happy and spend some time with her. I would pray throughout my life, but it was usually to thank God and show my gratitude for things in my life. I lit a candle, sat down in the middle of the church where they had seats set up in a semicircle, and I closed my eyes. I didn't think I had any tears left, but I started to cry, and I prayed. I did not pray to show gratitude, and I did not pray to ask for Tony to want to be with me or to make any of my pain go away. I actually felt like I was begging instead of praying.

"Dear God, the universe, Buddha, Mother Mary, Jesus, Papa, or anyone up there who is listening to me right now—please, please, please just give me strength. I don't know what I am going home to, but I really feel it is not good and that it is not going to be easy. Please give me strength to get through whatever this next chapter is for me. Please help me to be strong and help me to be okay. Please be someone or something that I can turn to, to know I am going to get through this. Please don't make this break me. This can't break me. Please bring Tony peace and strength too. Obviously, he is going through something, and I can't help him. He won't let me, but I wish he would. I trust you. I trust that whatever is happening is for a reason. I trust whatever is going to happen for me is the path I am supposed to be on. I trust you will get me through it. I trust it will all be okay. Please help me be okay, please. I don't even have to be happy, I just want to be okay. Thank you for listening. Sorry for asking for so much when I never really spoke to you like this before. Please watch over me. I love you and thank you."

It was true. I had a hard time picturing myself ever feeling happy again in the mental state I was currently in, and I desperately wanted to *not* feel the hurt and confusion I was currently feeling. Emma and I found each other, and we walked up the 528 steps to the dome of the church. Our legs were shaking from the strain, and the air felt so different up there. It was cold and fresh and we had a beautiful view of the entire city. It was the perfect way to end our trip.

After twelve hours of traveling, I was right when I knew whatever I was going home to was not good. After being away for thirteen days, Tony and I picked up where we left off—it was over. Desperate for some type of answer to the one-eighty that took place, I started looking for anything to make sense of what was going on, starting with our phone bill. That's when I found out there was in fact someone else.

In some ways it definitely was a relief because I knew I wasn't going mad, that was until the betrayal really kicked in. He had met someone else at the gym and no longer wanted to be in our marriage. There was nothing I could do about it.

Never in a million years did I think when I was picking out this Jacobean hardwood floor in our new bedroom that I would be curled up crying on it with my face pressed up against it. I picked myself up and went into survival mode. I packed up my trunk with all wedding-related things, extra favors, decorations, and my beautiful dress. I asked my mom to meet me at a Starbucks where I had to tell her what was going on. Hunched over our coffees and a small round table, I asked her to take everything away for me. From there, all I could focus on were the next steps.

I felt so alone. Weirdly alone. Knowing 50 percent of marriages end in divorce, I couldn't fathom how with a statistic like that, how I could feel this way. I didn't want this to be me. With this statistic, how can one still feel so alone while going through it? I truly felt like I was the only person who knew how I felt and that it was never going to get better, that I would never feel "normal" again. Yes, the technical part of getting divorced can be a nightmare itself. The coming to the realization that the relationship is beyond repair, that too much damage has been done, and that there is no coming back from it. Then there are the legalities of it and the actual separation of the life you had together. It was such a stressful time. I was on this roller coaster of emotions, but most of the time, I was just truly heartbroken. Wholeheartedly heartbroken. I remember packing up my house and evenly distributing the silverware and the dishes to make sure we both had enough to start over. That was only the beginning of the ride I was on.

I realized on this trip and through this experience that I had to focus on only the things I had control on in this situation. I couldn't obsess over why Tony was acting out or trying to change or make sense of what he had done and decided, no matter how much I wanted to. My life felt as if it was turned upside down, by someone else's actions, but it was my life and my responsibility to turn it back around.

LET'S CHECK IN

If you reflect on your situation right now, what is in your control? What is not?

Write that out or pause and think about it for a moment.

When you are able to regain control, you can shift perspective and start taking steps toward feeling clearer. It's those small steps that add up over time.

who I was after divorce

Divorce in itself is one thing, but there are so many parts of it that no one really talks about. Once it is all said and done, and you've moved out and closed that last bank account with both your names, and in my case, you find yourself sitting at a diner eating French onion soup alone, you start to mourn. You mourn the person you spent every single day with, whether they were good or bad. And when you think you've mourned it all, there's so much more than that. You mourn the routine you shared, the home you built together, the plans that you made, the children you may have planned to have, the holidays you've had together, the family you were married into, and everything—*everything*—in between. It is so much more than the loss of the actual person; you mourn the timeline you were once on, and it takes time to adjust and build back up.

My credit was shot because I put most of the renovation debt in my name. I already had student loans, so we decided to continue to add the debt to my name and keep Tony's perfect, allowing us to buy houses and flip them in the future. Emma scoped apartments for me during this time; I couldn't bring myself to do this. I didn't have the luxury of "moving back in with Mom and Dad" that many people have after they divorce. She narrowed it down to a few top picks and found one close by to see that night. I stood in the empty, bare one-bedroom basement apartment and couldn't believe that this is what my life was. I started crying and thought for sure I scared the landlord away with my meltdown and was convinced he didn't want some blond emotional head case living in his house. I called him that night, and he said he would be happy to give it to me. I was so grateful. He asked me to come the next day to sign the lease and give my security deposit, which Tony's brother Matt helped me with until I was able to get my finances in order. I had a decent job in the fashion industry, but I had a staggering amount of debt, and now I had to pay rent and all my bills on my own. My bills were way more than what I made, but I was determined I would figure it out, and I also counted on receiving some money once the house sold. The next day, I marched into my boss's office who I had a great relationship with. She was like a work mom to me and had been at my wedding. I don't know what happened, but I started crying. I asked her, "Please, can I have more money? I'll do more work, I'll work more hours, whatever you need me to do. I just really need it if I am going to keep working here." She didn't even ask me any questions. She gave me a hug and said, "I will see what I can do, and I'm here if you need anything." I was determined to take control of the little I had control over and try to make some changes, and my job was one of these things.

I painted the apartment the same gray tones I had picked in my last two houses and moved in. The first night was depressing and so strange. It was like a lonelier, smaller version of my old house. One of my oldest friends showed up with food and unpacked my whole closet for me while secretly tossing out clothes she thought were ugly. I was so thankful because I had pushed everyone away and insisted on doing it all by myself. Picking up the big U-Haul on my own and having it parked outside my house for hours for all of the neighbors to see was devastating. I was a zombie and couldn't be around anyone. I felt like I was being judged, and in some way, I felt I owed everyone something along with all of the other emotions I was dealing with. I didn't want to put anyone out; I was so embarrassed and ashamed asking anyone for anything, especially after my circus wedding only two months before. Situations like "Thanks for the overpriced KitchenAid you just got me. Can you come help me move it to my sad and lonely single girl apartment now?" made me feel like such a loser.

I had never lived alone in my whole life. I was the kid who wouldn't even stay over at friends' because I would get homesick. My dad would always pick me up in the middle of the night from sleepovers. Now here I was, in an apartment that didn't feel like mine. I didn't have couches or cable yet. I had all mismatched furniture, my bed and two chairs from my old house with a small old kitchen table that I had taken from the basement that Tony and I had in our first apartment. It was like a weird combination of every stage of the last ten years of my life. Thank God, I had my dog, Jess, with me. I got custody of her since she was a gift to me for my birthday. As much as Tony loved her, he wouldn't try to take her from me.

That first night I slept half the night with the light on after realizing I had hooked my TV up to the outlet that was attached to the light switch, and I needed the background noise to go to sleep. Finally, at 4 a.m., I woke up to take the lightbulb out of the fixture and completely broke it. The next day, I went to Home Depot to buy an extension cord and a new light. My dad came over that morning, brought me food, and spent the day with me. This became a weekly occurrence of him coming over and bringing me groceries. My ex-mother-in-law would check on me multiple times a day. She would bring me food and leave paper towels and toilet paper on my doorstep constantly. I was so grateful for her and the support I did have around me, but everyone feeling bad for me was not helping me feel any better about myself or the situation. I felt like such a victim, and it was the last role I wanted to play. Everyone was walking on eggshells around me, and it pushed me more into playing the "I'm fine" role.

I was on a tight budget and didn't have money for cable. Emma had given me her Netflix log-in, and I was able to use someone's Wi-Fi who lived nearby with a public account. I would stay up all night watching every episode of *Grey's Anatomy*, back-to-back from season one. I cried every episode. It was a nice way to release the feelings I was bottling up over McDreamy instead of what was really going on in my life.

I powered through my first week of being alone. I stared at myself in the bathroom mirror, bags under my eyes from the emotional battle I endured, and I didn't recognize one piece of myself. I had no idea who I was or where I was supposed to go from here. I didn't know exactly where I had lost myself over the years with Tony. It wasn't one big moment; it was little moments, little sacrifices over time that eventually added up into a version of myself who I didn't know. I couldn't picture ever feeling normal again. I felt like I had no true identity and had no idea what the fuck was next for me.

LET'S CHECK IN

These moments were hard. I won't sugarcoat it because I know now that I had to go through it to become stronger. Maybe you're in that place, binge-watching your favorite show too. One thing I do wish is that someone had dropped questions for me to think over during those times. Questions like these:

- Are you someone who enjoys being alone?
- What do you like about it?
- Do you have any fear surrounding being alone?
- What about it scares you?

rock bottom

When I was first single, I was in full-blown fight or flight mode. I had lists and lists of things I had to get done and jumped on any invite I received. I was so scared to slow down and actually be alone, be in my thoughts, and be in my new reality that I had no idea how to navigate. For about two years, instead of facing anything, I kept myself busy. The second I didn't have anything to do, I was reaching out to anyone and everyone to see if there was something or someone I could fill my time with. I brushed off the past and what had happened to me as if it didn't affect me. I put up a strong front because I didn't want to admit that I was broken, that someone else had the power to completely break me. I carried a lot of shame around this. It was hard for me to be home and not want to self-medicate by drinking my feelings away.

As much as I loved bingeing Netflix, I was incredibly lost. I honestly don't think I would still be here if I didn't have Jess. She gave me something that I had to take care of, a responsibility, and a purpose. I loved her more than not loving myself or liking my life at the time. She made sure I got out of the apartment and kept going. The love and affection a dog can show you, especially at your worst, is truly amazing. The number of times I would cry and she would jump up to my neck and lick all my tears away would instantly make me feel like I wasn't alone. She assured me that I wasn't. My cousins, who I have always had a good relationship with, started inviting me to dinner every single night. I became extremely close with my cousin's wife, Lana. She had been through something similar, and she took me under her wing, was a shoulder to cry on, and was someone who made me laugh until my stomach hurt.

Sundays had become hard because despite our opposite schedules, this was the one day Tony and I would sleep in, have sex, eat breakfast, and watch one of our shows. I didn't know what to do with myself. The small apartment took me an hour to clean, and with my dad bringing me dinners regularly, I was out of my element.

One night, I was sitting on my couch (which was finally

delivered) after work, drinking my usual wine, and eating sushi. I was going back and forth between scrolling on Instagram and swiping left and right on this new world of "dating" I now found myself in for the first time in my late twenties. I absolutely hated it. Don't get me wrong, I know plenty of friends and family who have had successful stories of meeting online, my cousin and Lana being examples, but it was not an easy or natural thing for me to get into. I also think I wasn't ready yet, as it hadn't been long since the crash of Tony and me.

I had come across an old friend's Instagram photo of her apartment, looking all cozy and cute, while mine still felt empty, cold, and like a shrine to my old life. I replied, "Love it! Where did you get that plant?"

She responded, "Home Goods. I hope you are doing well, babe. The pictures of the wedding looked beautiful!"

Doing well?! I thought, if people only knew what was really going on—I had to delete my Facebook account because people were still commenting on my wedding pictures that were posted.

This friend's name was Stefani, and we had known each other since we were thirteen. We would go from being good friends to drifting on and off throughout the years. We never had a fight or anything, but we would find ourselves in different relationships and circles of friends over the span of our fifteen-year friendship. The past five years we had not been in touch, but we always celebrated each other's lives through social media, and we loved and respected each other.

I responded back, "Thank you, let's catch up one day soon. I have a lot to tell you. xo"

She replied instantly. "I'm going out tomorrow with a few friends. Why don't you come meet me?"

"Sounds good, I'll text you," I responded, feeling so grateful in that moment. I felt that my family didn't really know how to be around me. I know everyone was just as heartbroken as I was. I knew where it was coming from, but everyone was treating me like a wine glass that was filled to the tippy top, with a crack in it that was about to shatter or spill at any sudden movement. People would say, "At least you didn't have kids yet."

And I would think, *Yeah, I guess.* I know divorce with kids involved is ten times harder, but geez, I was still dealing with the loss of him, and I was truly alone now. I almost wish I had a kid out of the deal! I had lost almost all of my "friends" through my breakup, and I say "friends" because not one of the girls in our group even reached out throughout all of this. The girls I had surrounded myself with and welcomed as my friends for ten years clearly were never my friends. I understand when people break up it is natural that relationships change and shift, but Tony and I were not on bad terms. I did nothing wrong.

My sister-in-law Tina and I remain close to this day. We talk on a weekly basis, and we'll be there for each other in a minute if the other needs. Yes, our relationship had to change, but she was there for me every step of the way and still is, while being respectful to Tony and her family.

I met up with Stefani the next night and we picked up right where we left off. We caught each other up on the last few years, and it turned out she was newly single also. It was fate that we reconnected at this time. Our apartments were right down the block from each other, and we immediately started doing everything together and have been inseparable ever since. Instead of watching *Sex and the City* and *Titanic* and drinking tea while my mom would make us brownies, like we did when we were sixteen, we were going out to dinners every night, drinking dirty martinis, having dance parties in our apartments, and watching Bravo. Stefani welcomed me into her group of friends, and little did I know at that time, but I was meeting two people who would one day become my best friends, Justin and Nicole. This was a group of people that I likely wouldn't have found myself having in my life had I still been in my marriage. A lot of times in the movies, it's a new hot neighbor who comes and saves you, but in my case, it was these friendships. It felt so refreshing to start connecting with people who were not linked to my old life. Stefani, Nicole, and Justin were all single, and we were exactly who we all needed at that time.

Despite my newfound friend group, I was still masking what was going on in my life with Tony. I put on this whole—*everything happens for a reason*—confident front for everyone, but I could not wrap my head around the turn that had taken place in my life. I still had hope that he would come to me at any moment and give me what I needed. As much as I was done and knew I deserved better, I still had a hard time letting go of all the good we had and the life that I had mapped out for us. There was still a part of me that really wanted to make things work between us. I focused on all the good we had and didn't think about the bad. I was doing anything to not feel. I kept covering up my pain with a Band-Aid, but the wound kept festering and the poison was spreading. I pushed down everything I was feeling and wouldn't deal with any of it. I was so stressed about money and everything else that was going on, I had no idea how I was ever going to recover from the financial mess I was in. I had received the raise I had asked for, but it still wasn't enough to keep up with my bills. I was drinking excessively every single night from the minute I got home from work until I passed out. I was smoking weed and taking Xanax when I couldn't sleep. I would wake up groggy, miserable, and terribly hungover and would get through my days by taking Tylenol; eating bacon, egg, and cheeses; and drinking coffee all day only to do it again the next. I had a nine-to-five job in the city with a ninety-minute commute each way. Beyond exhausted, depressed, and so very broken, I was abusing my body badly. What's funny is that I was down twenty pounds from the stress of everything and people would say, "You look great!"

Yeah, I'd think while being tortured inside, *my husband cheated on me and left me for a girl he met at the gym, and I throw up every single morning from drinking a bottle of wine every night, but thanks!* I felt like I was an empty shell existing only for the chaos, and I didn't even know who I was anymore. I couldn't slow down and face or feel what was really going on in my life. As much as I was spreading myself thin, I couldn't stop. I needed to feel something other than the loneliness, pain, and fear that I was consumed with. I had tried cocaine for the first time during this period, which could have been a game changer for me and how my life could have gone. The first time I did it, I had no idea what I was doing and ended up blowing it all over the entire car instead. Thankfully, I didn't like it. I was always a good girl and never did anything "bad" before. In high school, when all of my friends were experimenting with weed and pain pills, I would just sit there slowly sipping my Twisted Tea in the corner. I loved my sleep, so uppers didn't do it for me. The mixing of the wine and the Xanax did, however. There were plenty of nights that I blacked out and didn't remember what went on the night before. Most of these times I was home and "safe," but it still didn't make it okay. It was clear that I was numbing everything I was feeling, and I was on a downward spiral, fast. I knew this wasn't the person I wanted to be.

LET'S CHECK IN

It didn't happen overnight, but I was able to slowly pull myself out of these destructive patterns I found myself in. The first step was to become aware of them. If you feel yourself going down a similarly destructive path, start by thinking of one thing that helps you feel better when you are down that is healthy for you. It doesn't have to be big. Is it going for a walk? Listening to music? Drinking water?

Becoming aware of this clearly points out what you are doing that does not align with where you want to be. Can you make it a point to do it every day? Once it becomes a part of your daily routine, can you add something else? Then something else? This was how I did it:

- I started with waking up every morning and journaling at least five things I was grateful for.

- I then added five minutes of meditation music, which eventually led to ten to fifteen, to sometimes more than thirty minutes.

- I made sure to get outside for at least thirty minutes a day, even if it meant just sitting in my yard.

These may not seem like big moves, but over time, they made a big difference.

why did I still care?

There was a point when time had passed, but Tony and I were still communicating, mostly about bills, the house, and plans going forward. I missed Tony terribly and wanted nothing more than to be back in our home together before any of this had happened. I constantly worried about him, actually—he was someone I took care of for so long and now I couldn't figure out how to turn that off. Some of my friends thought I was nuts to be sad for him after everything he had done to bring us into this situation. They would say, "I wish I could be in your head for just one day."

I couldn't help it, though. I imagined he was feeling everything I was feeling, but he had to know that he was the one to cause it. People were mad at him, and I took that on. I felt bad about it; I somehow felt it was my fault. Yes, I was angry and hurt, but I was also confused and still cared about him. He had come across some medical issues and had to get surgery shortly after I had moved out. He'd had a bad stomach, and the stress of our situation, I would think, pushed it to the next level. We were broken up, living separately, but I couldn't physically *not go* to the hospital and be by his side while this went on. Again, people didn't understand—even he didn't, really—but it was the only thing that felt natural to me and that was all that mattered.

There is no rule book when it comes to breaking up and divorce. It is not the same for everyone, and it is definitely not a flat road. What makes sense for you may not make sense for others—and that is okay. I was his caretaker for so long. It was the role I had held for years. In fact, it was a role I had held for a lot of people around me—taking care of others at the expense of myself—and it was a very hard habit to stop.

There were plenty of ups and downs the months following me moving out. There were the obvious things like bills and selling the house, but it was the small things that seemed to make the most impact. I had never had to get my car inspected before or knew how to put air in my tires; he had handled that for so long. Tony didn't know any of the logins for all of our accounts and had never washed sheets in his life, so I had to show him how. These were all very normal things we had to navigate through. As mad and confused as I was, I missed him equally and was trying to make this process go as smoothly as possible.

There was a short period when he was trying to get back together and attempted to repair what had been broken. I had already moved out. It was a few weeks away from Emma's wedding. To say I was having a difficult time entertaining this idea would be an understatement. I had made excuses for him in our whole relationships for certain behavior, and I had come to the realization that I couldn't make an excuse for what he did. Twenty-five days after saying our vows, two weeks after our honeymoon, a lifetime of promises were gone. Deep down, he didn't really want me no matter how much he wanted to, and we both knew it.

In the midst of these conversations we would have, I walked into my empty apartment one day, with Jess greeting me, of course, and looked around. I looked at this little life I had built for myself in this short period of time and felt a glimpse of pride. I didn't want to leave this place I had created. This space was filled with some of my saddest and loneliest times, but it was also filled with the most independence I had ever had. I couldn't go backward, even with Tony trying to show me how sorry he was. The thought of going back to that house and back to the broken place we would be in was something I didn't want. I didn't want to have a pit in my stomach if I heard his phone go off or if he came home late one night or if he snapped at me for something silly like he had in the past. I decided I did not want that life for myself. I knew I didn't deserve to be treated like that by anyone. I treated him like the king of the castle. I would cut his toenails for him, for fuck's sake! We were at our high and that's when he cheated on me and made me feel like it was my fault. He lied and betrayed me at this time. *What would he do when I was nine months pregnant and sixty pounds overweight?*

I knew I would never truly be able to be happy with him ever again, and I decided for the first time ever that I wanted better for myself. I sat there on my small gray sectional, full of emotion. I wish I had felt different. I wish I was more confident in coming back better than ever because I have heard stories like that in the past, but my intuition was strong and was telling me this was not the way to go in my situation. It was screaming at me, and I couldn't ignore it if I tried. I had to be done, and for the first time in my life, I had to choose myself and the potential of how happy I could be. During those last three months, I did have time to look back and reflect on our relationship and there were things I was not okay with.

Once he cheated, everything changed. I knew I was strong, I knew I would be okay, but I was his rock. He said it himself constantly. He wasn't going to have me anymore, and it broke my heart. At the end of the day, I knew I didn't want to be with someone who didn't want to be with me; someone who would risk losing me so easily. I would never have cheated on Tony. I had never lied or flirted or even looked at anyone else when I was with him. I wanted a partner who felt like that toward me. I wanted someone who would put me on a pedestal and who never in a million years would hurt or betray me the way that he did. I wanted someone who was so scared of losing me, not someone who was impulsive at the first chance they got. I questioned myself all week—*was I doing the right thing?* I kept replaying our last conversation. I wondered if I had made the biggest mistake, not agreeing to go back. I had such a hard time trusting myself. Later that week on Instagram, I saw that he was back with the twenty-something-year-old from the gym. There was my answer. They have been together ever since.

I could have chosen hate and negativity and tried to take him for everything he had, but I didn't. Sending him and the gym girl those angry texts the day I found out about the affair made me not like myself, and I didn't want to go back to that. That energy would have only been negative to me and my body, and I decided to choose love and forgiveness instead. There were plenty of moments when I wanted to knock on her door when I saw his truck outside and embarrass them in front of her parents and neighbors, but that wouldn't have changed anything. I still would have been hurt and on my own. It was not always easy, but in the end, I am happy that this is the route I chose.

LET'S CHECK IN

One tool that helped me navigate this emotional time was checking in with myself when reacting to things and asking, Will this change the outcome?

Most of the time, the answer was no. I truly believe starting this dialogue with yourself will help you heal and start to move on.

survival mode

The summer of 2017 and my sister Emma's wedding was right around the corner. I hated the thought that my situation had affected her and her day in any way. I mean, how could it not? She had recently stood next to me as I said my vows and got married only to witness it all fall apart less than thirty days later. Now, she was about to do the same, and I felt terrible that all of this was on her mind during what was supposed to be the happiest time of her life.

"Dom is not Tony; this will not happen to you." I said it to her so fiercely and confidently, but how the hell did I know? I put on my trusty emotional armor, buried my feelings down, and stayed positive and excited for my dear sister. Genuinely thrilled to be her maid of honor, I did my best.

A week before the wedding, we had gone to lunch and to her last dress fitting. I walked into the boutique and suddenly my legs felt like they wouldn't be able to hold me up. The last time I was there was when I had picked up my dress. All the girls who worked there had known what happened (Staten Island really is a small town). I started using a mechanism where I would visualize swallowing tears that weren't there yet to prevent them from pouring out. *Swallow the tears, swallow the tears, swallow the tears,* I would say over and over in my head until they went away. *Phew*, I thought, *that was close to a full meltdown.*

Emma looked absolutely beautiful in her dress. She really was the most beautiful bride I had ever seen in my life. The genuine smile that lit up her face could make the saddest person light up with joy, and at that point, it was me. We left the store, and she couldn't stop talking about how happy she was and how she couldn't wait to see Dom's face when he saw her in her dress. She was on cloud nine, and even though I was happy for her, I felt myself falling apart while she was talking. All I could picture was Tony seeing me for the first time in my dress and how he started sobbing and how it was real—I knew it was. *How are we here?* I kept asking myself while trying to stay focused on Emma. *It's not about you, Case, it's not about you. Pull it the fuck together*.

Thankfully, I had my huge sunglasses on, and I kept nodding and letting out a random and excited, "I know!" Driving quicker than usual because I knew I couldn't contain the tears much longer, I dropped her off and gave her a hug as she got out of the car, pulled away and turned down the next block. As soon as I could, I pulled over and lost it. All the tears and emotions that I was holding in regarding the wedding and everything going on came out of the floodgates. I was sobbing and in so much pain. I called my aunt, who I often did in these times, and cried thoroughly. I barely said anything coherent, and lovingly she listened and, as always, was there to be my shoulder to cry on. I felt blameworthy and guilty for feeling sad about my own mess. This wasn't about me; it was about Emma. It was difficult to navigate the jadedness I felt and the joy I had for her and to separate the two.

On the morning of Emma's big day, the excitement level was every bit that you could imagine. She was so relaxed and calm, and the energy was contagious to everyone else. I couldn't wait to celebrate Emma and Dom. Yes, I could've done without seeing half of my family members that day (the last time I saw them I was in the big white dress), but I tried not to give it any thought or energy. I was the skinniest and probably the unhealthiest I'd ever been in my life, but I felt great putting on my dress. In hindsight, when I look at those pictures, I know it was because I was eating an apple a day and the rest of my calories were alcohol. I don't know if it was nerves, but I kept eating donuts and my dress ended up snapping right before we left! For the rest of the day, Nanny kept telling everyone: "Casey ate five donuts this morning, and her dress broke right before we left, and I had to fix it!"

I was the maid of honor, so I was the last to walk down the aisle right before my dad and Emma. As we were standing in the vestibule, I couldn't help but feel some PTSD because Dad and I had just done this a few months earlier. It was intensely emotional being happy for the two of them in that moment while also having flashbacks of my dad walking me down the aisle and handing me off to Tony. I started tearing up as I was cued to start walking. *I definitely didn't think this moment through.* I knew I was the maid of honor, and I knew I would be walking down the aisle by myself, but holy shit, universe! My entire family was all looking at me, smiling and thinking, "Aw, you've got this," similar to the way you look at the picture of the abused puppies on the can at a deli counter and you put the dollar in not knowing if it's doing much, but you want to be supportive anyway. Despite it all, it was a memorable event I would pick to relive again and again if I had the chance.

LET'S CHECK IN

Here are some healthy ways I learned to cope during these times:

- I surrounded myself with people who loved me and wanted the best for me. If I didn't have that at a moment, I made sure to be that person for myself.
- I let go of judgment and the fear surrounding what others thought of me. I realized what happened to me was not a reflection of me.
- I focused on where I wanted to be in my life, how I wanted to feel moving forward opposed to where I was in the past, and how I felt.
- It was hard work but not impossible—and you can do this too. One day at a time.

acceptance

The summer had passed, and I was in the acceptance stage of life. I knew I was no longer the girl who I was in my marriage, but I knew I wasn't the person I was turning into either. The depression was still there, even when I didn't realize it. While I was growing up, when my mom was depressed, she would stay in bed all day. I knew I didn't want to do that. I got up for work and made myself clean and tidy the apartment, visit friends, and go on with my life. The minute I would get home, however, I would crawl into bed, or the second I was alone, I would cry.

I was depressed, functioning still, but utterly hollow at times inside. I never had suicidal thoughts but would often go to sleep at night thinking how completely okay I would be if I never woke up. I had gone from someone hiding behind my relationship and lacking any self-love to being this new version of myself with a full-blown sentiment of self-hatred. I couldn't believe how replaceable I felt. How was Tony able to meet someone, who in his eyes was better than me, and within a week throw our whole life out the window? I felt like I wasn't good enough for anyone. I felt like everyone around me was judging me.

I'd heard that when someone is cheated on one of the first questions asked is, "Well, did they do something to deserve it?" It's a bullshit question. Regardless of what is going on between two people, there is never a reason to lie and be unfaithful. I was now carrying around this unwanted badge and felt I needed to explain myself all the time that I didn't "deserve" this. I felt I had something to prove. I was finding validation from having sex with all of the wrong guys. I was only entertaining emotionally and physically unavailable people. Seriously, the more unavailable they were, the better. Getting deployed? Getting back with your ex? Going to jail? Fresh out of a relationship? Still live with your wife? Sure, I'll hang out with you. I was doing this because I knew it wasn't going to go anywhere, so I wouldn't get hurt again. The thought of starting anything serious with anyone ever again consumed me with PTSD. Engaging with these guys who were all wrong for me kept me in a safe place where I wouldn't get attached yet still felt wanted by someone. I would criticize myself constantly. I was filled with so much hurt and anger. I started to believe the narrative in my head and felt like I had deserved everything that happened to me. Maybe if I had been a better wife or if I had been more confident, Tony wouldn't have left me for someone else. I felt I didn't deserve anyone or a healthy relationship.

I was in this cycle for a few months. It took me a while to realize that our thoughts are a strong and powerful tool, and they are what we truly can control. The things that we think and say to ourselves influence our mood, our self-worth, and the energy we are giving ourselves, and in turn, what we are putting out into the universe. I started becoming aware of this negative self-talk I was having with myself and realized, *I would never say these things to my worst enemy. I wouldn't even repeat them out loud! So why was I saying them to myself?*

The truth was I was enough, I was not replaceable, and I was worthy. Nothing I could have done would have changed our outcome, and those are the things I started speaking to myself.

Journal entry—August 2, 2017

I am so angry lately. I hate the second. It's so hard to think Tony and I would be celebrating anniversaries on this day, and we never even were able to celebrate one month. If he would have done the right thing, we would have been seven months into therapy by now, and it makes me sick to my stomach. I hate him for taking my life away from me and for the person I am becoming. I will never understand why he did this, and it makes me so sad. I hate thinking that I should have pushed him more for answers or to go to therapy with me, but he kept shutting me out and pushing me away. I don't know. I really don't think there was anything else I could have done. I did try a lot. I'm sick of being so sad and want it all behind me.

This past weekend I got drunker than I have ever been. I fell in the bathtub and really hurt my arm. I am so tired of being sad and thinking how my life used to be versus where it is now. I just want to be happy again and not be confused and sad anymore. I just pray for the day that I wake up and don't think of him or have that knot in my stomach. I feel like it is never going to go away. I never would have thought my life would be so messed up and this is who I would be. I will try to be better tomorrow.

Emma and Dom had gone to Italy on their honeymoon and announced they were pregnant shortly after. Emma actually told me before she even told Dom, and I was beyond excited! I love kids so much! Lana had two little girls, six months old, who I spent a lot of time with, and I was so happy that Emma and Lana would have kids who would be cousins around the same age. I was spending more and more time with my cousins. I often felt like the adopted child, as they had big families and plans of their own, and Emma was now starting hers as well. I felt like there were two sides of me. The side that was babysitting and having dance parties with all of the kids in my family, and the side that would sit on my couch alone at night filled up with so much negativity. I started going to therapy to deal with depression and self-hate. I went through a few people before I found someone I really clicked with, but regardless, it felt great to be able to just talk about what was going on to a third party without any judgment.

As fall ended and my once favorite season started to begin, I couldn't help but be overwhelmed with anxiety and sadness over the one-year mark coming up. I felt like September to December of the past year was literally the happiest time of my life, before it all fell apart. It was my bridal shower, fall, Thanksgiving in our new home, our wedding, our honeymoon, and Christmas right before my life was shaken around like a fucking snow globe where none of the pieces are glued down right. What would have been our one-year anniversary fell on a Saturday that year. As I was leaving work Friday, my boss pulled me into her office before I left for the day and asked me to shut the door. This is the same boss I was crying in front of a year earlier telling her that my marriage was falling apart. *Shit, I'm definitely getting fired*, I thought. All this time, I've been thinking I've been keeping my shit together and no one had noticed me being a hungover mess every day and off my game, but obviously she has. *Fuck my life.*

She began the conversation in a surprising way. "So, I know tomorrow would have been your anniversary. What are your plans?"

"Ahh." I sighed with relief, along with thoughts of *How the hell did she remember?* "I plan on just relaxing and waiting for the day to be over. Thank you so much for asking. I really appreciate you so much," I meaningfully replied.

"Since it's still new this year, I'm only suggesting this for next year, but I need you to make a new memory on this day, so you have something else to resonate it with." She shared with me that this is what she started to do after her husband had died years earlier.

Was she really comparing my cheating husband to the death of her husband and the father of her children?! Geez, I felt like such a loser. I told her I liked the idea, and I would keep it in mind for the next year. She gave me a big hug, and I left for the day. She really was like my work mom, and I was so grateful for her support.

The next day, I had my phone on "Do Not Disturb." It was one of those mornings when you wake up with a giant pit in your stomach before you even open your eyes. I had an internal dialogue with myself while still half asleep. "No, don't open your eyes, don't look at your phone, don't check the time, don't see the date December second on your screen. Stay asleep. Do not get up!"

I'd had far too many of these mornings over the past year, but this one was particularly intense. I would pray every day for the day that I would wake up and not be thinking of Tony. I would pray all of the time, "Please let me go through just one day without thinking of him, just one day where I do not cry."

But I felt like that day would never come no matter how much time went on. I glanced at my phone as Jess woke me up with kisses. I couldn't even read through all of the "thinking of you today" messages I had received. Ugh, again, I felt like such a failure, but I recognized I had such amazing people in my corner. Lana would abso-lutely not accept that I wanted to be alone that day and hunker down and just let it pass like a fucking hurricane. She insisted that we go out for lunch. I reluctantly agreed and pulled it together. I knew she would be right there in my small, dark, depressing chamber of an apartment with me the entire day if I didn't.

We went for lunch, and I started with a dirty martini and she with a Cosmo on our very empty stomachs. We sat at a restaurant on the water, decorated beautifully for Christmas as we talked for hours, reflecting on the past year, cried multiple times, laughed until our stomachs hurt, and before we knew it, we were completely drunk at 2:30 in the afternoon. We really did have a great time together. I hadn't heard from Tony that day, and as much as I didn't want to, it was one of those texts that you keep looking at your phone to see if you are going to get. I was still pretending to be strong in front of most people, but Lana was someone I could be vulnerable with, and I couldn't have pictured spending the day with anyone else.

When I got home later that night, still pretty drunk, I stumbled to my door and noticed something on my stoop—flowers from Tony. The card read: "Hope this brightens up your day a little."

My heart dropped, and I sobbed myself to sleep. I had texted Lana the next day thanking her for lunch and for the good time we had despite the cloud over the day.

She replied saying, "It's our anniversary now!" I didn't plan on it, but I did make a new memory that day, and every year since then, Lana and I now go out for dinner, just the two of us, for our anniversary! I had survived my first holiday season divorced and alone.

Emma had snuck into my house on Christmas Eve and left me gifts from Santa since it was going to be my first Christmas morning alone. My parents and my sister all invited me to come stay with them, but everything was different now. My parents were separated, my childhood home no longer there to go home to, Kelsey and Danny lived on their own, and Emma and Dom were spending their first Christmas morning together as a married couple. I was divorced and single and I accepted it, deciding to stay home. As I got up that morning, I made a huge cup of tea, opened my presents, cuddled with Jess, and watched my favorite movie, *The Holiday*. I was committed more than ever to start making new memories of my own. I spent that New Year's Eve alone with a bottle of wine and a facemask, falling asleep by 10 p.m., thinking how relieved I was that 2017 was over.

LET'S CHECK IN

My New Year Reflections Art Project!

I make this into an art project yearly and gently suggest it for you as well. I use fun colors, light a candle, and take the time to reflect on the last year. By doing this, I become aware of where I am at versus where I want to be. Then I head into the New Year intentionally. This can be done a few times a year or whenever you want or feel it will be helpful. It is one of my favorite New Year's traditions, and I look forward to it every year.

CHALLENGES	TRIUMPHS

WHAT WORKED	WHAT DIDN'T WORK

MOST SUCCESS	FELL SHORT

dating

Dating for the first time in my thirties was eye-opening for me. I didn't even know what I liked and what I didn't like. If someone asked me what I did for fun, the first thing that would come to my mind was, "I have been planning my wedding for the last two years and had zero social life. I like going to Home Goods on the weekends to decorate my house."

Now, I was in this small apartment and didn't have an inch of room anywhere to put another piece of furniture or hang something on the wall. I genuinely enjoyed cleaning and hosting and playing house, but I knew I couldn't put that in my dating profile!

Despite being ready to date or not, swiping left and

right on an app felt so unnatural to me. It was like a creepy game of "Guess Who" where you would wonder if the person you would swipe right on would choose you back. It was not exciting for me; it was actually pretty depressing.

Apparently, even though it made me uncomfortable, this was the only way to date these days, and I hated everything about it. It felt like a job, like a lot of work and a lot of effort for someone I didn't even know if I had a natural connection with, because how could I? Everyone had a limitless number of options just one swipe away. Putting so much time and thought into a conversation just to randomly get an unwarranted dick pic in the middle of "Hey, how was your day?" was just not for me. Online dating was not beneath me or anything, and I do believe it is a great way for two people who may not have crossed paths otherwise to interact and possibly turn a swipe into a relationship. I would spend hours of my life swiping left and right, thinking of the perfect first line to send, but 99 percent of the time, there was not a genuine connection, and I wasn't about to force it. I was still working long hours in the city, and I valued my time. I thought how much I would rather be on my couch with my dog or with my family and friends than out with a guy, who when I asked his nationality, gave me an hour-long mathematical breakdown of his ancestry.com report, or the guy who said he was a gourmet chef, only to find out he worked at Chipotle (not to knock Chipotle, but just don't lie about it!).

The number of people I matched with who ended up having girlfriends or wives or who turned out to be nothing like they portrayed themselves to be was mind-boggling and definitely not great for my trust issues.

The worst part was that I started defining my worth by these apps. How could total strangers make me feel a certain way about myself? *Is it because my teeth look bad in that picture? Should I have not used that emoji? Shit, I didn't mean to put an exclamation point there.*

I would take these conversations, or lack thereof, so personally that these total strangers would affect my mood and my self-confidence. I started to think the guys who I thought had potential thought I wasn't good enough when they didn't answer or disappeared. I came across two categories of men: the guys who wanted to interview me to be a wife (no thank you!) and the guys who were asking for my address right away to send me in an Uber to their house in the middle of the night. There was no in-between at all. I just wanted to date—old-school dating. I was done with having meaningless sex to fill a void. I wanted to go out and meet someone for a drink or coffee and see where it went. I was looking for a guy who would give me a little more of a plan than a "WYD" at 2 a.m., but not someone who was asking me when my lease was up two weeks in. Was that too much to ask? I felt like it was, and I started to give up. *Like what the actual fuck is this life that I am now in?!* Just a year prior, I'd been thinking what month would be a good time to start trying to have a baby based on the maternity clothes I liked better, fall or summer? And now here I was, swiping away on my couch, not able to find one person I could tolerate enough to go out on a second date with. It ended up becoming very discouraging for me, and I didn't want to do it anymore. I deleted the dating apps and gave into the idea that if I was meant to meet someone naturally, that was how I was going to meet them.

I realized that when I was dating because I felt I was supposed to, it was a negative experience for me. I hated that I felt I had to have a response to people when they would so often ask, "Did you find someone yet?" So, I would date just to date. Eventually, I did get to a place when I was dating because I authentically wanted to.

I changed my mindset when it came to dating and my role in all of my relationships to set the tone for what I wanted. If I met someone and they were looking to get married very fast, and it was something I was not ready for, I communicated that and didn't pursue it anymore. In the past, I would have clung to anyone who gave me this sense of safety or companionship. Or if I met someone who clearly just wanted a casual sexual relationship, if it wasn't something I wanted at the time, I stopped entertaining it. This prevented me from being in those confusing dating cycles we all find ourselves in. Many times, the other person is upfront about what they want or are looking for, and we as humans are conditioned to ignore any red flags and make up scenarios in our heads that "they will change" or "maybe they didn't mean it" or even worse "I am different." We completely set ourselves up for disappointment and failed relationships by not listening to people when they are straight-out telling us or showing us who they are and what they are looking for.

It was a Tuesday night and I was looking forward to having drinks I had lined up with someone I met naturally. I felt positive about it until I received a text that afternoon saying he had to cancel because he was stuck at work. As I read the text, I felt a sense of disappointment wash over me. The old me would have spiraled into:

- *He is lying.*
- *Every guy is the same.*
- *I am never going to meet anyone.*
- *Was it something I did or said?*

Chances are, yes, he could have been lying and had no intention of going out, but it had nothing to do with me. The new me changed my thought process and stopped letting any canceled date or form of rejection define me. Instead, I chose this:

- *He could be lying, or he could really be stuck at work.*
- *This has nothing to do with my self-worth.*
- *If he asks to reschedule, it is up to me if I want to do that.*
- *What do I get to order in and watch tonight?*

LET'S CHECK IN

It took time for me to get to this place, for me to learn and accept that other people's actions did not define me as a person. Especially after getting cheated on, you feel like you are not enough. At the end of the day, my actions define the person that I am, and the choices I make reflect me. If I decided to cancel a date and ghost someone, that reflects on me not being capable of being vulnerable and communicating with the other person. If this was done to me, I know that is not the type of person I would be interested in anyway.

Are you ready to make a mindset shift list?

Make a list like I did and see where you can reframe what you're thinking to take you into the mindset of "I am responsible for how I respond to this."

codependency

I grew up in a very codependent household, where boundaries were nonexistent. Don't get me wrong, some of my favorite childhood memories are of my mom enforcing family game night no matter what anyone had going on, or coming home to a house full of balloons on Valentine's Day because it was my parents' anniversary. I would wake up on Sundays to the smell of fried meatballs and my dad blasting Sinatra in the kitchen. We had Sunday dinners every week, no exceptions, and my parents, siblings, grandma, aunt, and uncle came together constantly to celebrate every little win any of us had. When it was good, this was a great dynamic, but when it was bad, it was a toxic environment. I learned at a young age what an empath was. I didn't know it back then, but I had a really hard time disconnecting from my family and any drama that went on. If Emma was upset because she received a bad grade, I would spend the whole night trying to make her feel better. If my parents were fighting, I would endlessly take it on and try to fix it between them. When any of this was going on, the entire energy in our household would dramatically change. Everyone was so codependent on one another that it led into all of us having a very inconsistent dynamic. I never knew what I was coming home to. Was it the happy family having a movie night, or was everyone in their rooms with the doors closed? I carried these inconsistencies into my adult relationships. After Tony and I were over, I swore I would never find myself in that dynamic again, putting someone's emotions first at the expense of my mental health.

My first relationship after my divorce tested me more than I knew possible. I thought I was invincible to ever being hurt again, but geez, was I wrong! I don't know if I will ever love anyone the way I loved Tony because it was so innocent and pure that I didn't have one wall up with him. As we grow older, our experiences shape us and teach us that boundaries make relationships healthier in the end—but not walls.

I met Jay about a year after my divorce, and I still was not interested in starting anything serious with anyone.

I had met him one night out at a bar with some friends, and we had clicked right away. We ended up dating on and off for a few years. Jay was tall and slender with light hair and light eyes, the physical opposite of Tony and of anyone I'd been attracted to in the past. We spent the entire night talking and laughing, and it ended with us drunkenly making out outside on the street corner. Our relationship went full speed ahead, fast. The first night we hung out one-on-one, about a week after our drunken bar night, we ended up sitting outside looking at the moon until 3 a.m. talking about everything you can imagine. We were instantly comfortable with each other and openly communicated as if we had known each other our whole lives. I connected with him on a spiritual level, one that I didn't have with Tony. I didn't feel an ounce of judgment come from him in all the conversations we had. We were constantly texting and on the phone and spending mul-tiple nights a week together. We were mutually obsessed with each other, physically and emotionally. Jay showed me a connection, a type of affection, and respect that I'd never had in my entire life. He spoke to me like I was his equal, admired me, and put me on a pedestal. I couldn't get enough of it. He made me feel like there was nothing wrong with me, and after being cheated on, betrayed, and left for someone else, you can only imagine how I clung to this feeling and to this person. He was passionate, sweet, and vulnerable, and it was so refreshing given the awful Bumble conversations I had found myself in (e.g., "Umm, I'd really like to continue talking, but first can you send me a better picture showing your whole body? Make sure your legs are in there too!").

As connected as we were, it was an extremely codependent relationship. He would never fully commit to me, which I pretended to be okay with. We had unbelievable sexual chemistry, which ended up becoming a large part of our relationship. They always say too much of anything isn't good, and that was the case for us. I almost became addicted to sex and felt that it validated me in some way because *someone wanted me* the way he did. We were like magnets and couldn't keep our hands off each other no matter where we were. I would ask myself all the time: *Is this what lust feels like, or do I love this person? Do I love the way he makes me feel, or do I feel like this because I love him? Does he really love me, or does he just love the way that I make him feel?* We couldn't get it right outside of our perfect bubble we created staying in, drinking wine while eating sushi, and having sex. I would wonder if we were both filling a void for each other that our previous partners didn't. No matter how hard we tried, and how hard we fought for it, it just didn't work. The intense feelings we had toward each other turned into erratic ups and downs of jealousy and codependency. It was very toxic behavior. In my previous relationship, Tony couldn't care less if I kept in touch with him, but with Jay, if a certain amount of time went by when I didn't reach out, it would result in a full-blown argument. Anytime I felt I was being questioned or doing anything out of obligation, I would lash out and pull away. Many of our arguments arose because, in his eyes, my clothes were now too revealing. I became terrified of slowly losing who I really was or what I wanted in a man again. I would overreact to conflict, instead of avoiding it like I had done for so long, and he gave it right back to me. He would say that I was cold, and it made me feel bad because he was right. I was no longer the girl who cried over everything. It takes so much to make me cry now! I had hardened after what I had been through, and I no longer was that sensitive girl that I always prayed not to be, but I didn't like it. Tony took that from me, and it made me mad that I let him.

As much as Jay would drop anything for me at any moment and was there for me through some of my hardest times, the fighting was nonstop. Again, I was programmed to accept unacceptable behavior because when people do bad things, it means they are hurting. I was in this constant battle in my head of what I knew I had to do versus what I was actually doing. I had a hard time not going back to him no matter how many times I said I was done. It was another very inconsistent relationship that I was oozing snippets of myself for. It was a true test to me, especially since I was trying so incredibly hard to break away from these patterns and find happiness within myself.

We were on this roller coaster for a while. I see now that we both had work and healing to do on our own before we could have a chance in the real world, but he made a strong impact on me regarding relationships and the qualities I want in a partner. He made me realize how I want to be loved and the feelings I would one day hold out for. He embraced every single part of me, even parts that I didn't like. One time, Jay and I were hanging out and I was playing with my hair in front of my face like I always did, and he grabbed my chin, pulled my hair back behind my ears, looked right in my eyes, and said, "Why do you always pull your hair in front of your face? Your face is so beautiful, and I can't see it when you cover it with your hair."

I felt like I was having an out-of-body experience. Tony *hated* how I looked with my hair up or back. He would always tell me to get my hair out from behind my ears. I didn't realize that after ten years being with this person who didn't like it, I was naturally conditioned to constantly pull my hair forward. Sounds like such a small and silly thing, right?! But for me it was *huge*. What else had I been unknowingly doing or not doing without real-izing it? Tony hated when I wore red lipstick, so I never even considered it. We would only drink white wine, so I never realized how much I love red. I have the worst allergies and would constantly have sneezing attacks, which he found very annoying, and now I find myself still apologizing every single time I sneeze. I started to think about these things. What was I doing because I wanted to versus what I was programmed to do after being with the same person for so long? Jay made me feel so easy to love, at a point when I felt so unbelievably unlovable, but it would have easily become another relationship where I defined my worth and my value based on the person I was with. My little pal, intuition, was speaking up louder than ever telling me I had to be completely on my own and heal myself before I could give any part of me to another person, and so we ultimately stopped seeing each other.

This relationship showed me patterns that I was very much caught up in. I became that people pleaser again, extremely codependent, and putting others' needs and wants in front of my own. I did fall in love with him, but it was more because of the potential of the relationship as opposed to what it actually was. I realized over time that this is what I had to focus on. I started only listening to those actions and following what was being done by the other person and realized it was never going to be what I once thought it would be.

If you find yourself in a dynamic with someone who you know is unhealthy or is bringing out a part of you that you don't necessarily like, take a step back from it. Realize that you are a part of the dynamic also. And by you removing yourself, it simply cannot go on. Instead of obsessing or putting your effort into changing someone, like I was for a while, focus on changing yourself and the role you play.

Change yourself first, and it may not be the outcome you think you want, but ultimately that shift alone will change the existing dynamic. In relationships, I found myself becoming introverted and avoiding conflict at all costs until my emotions bottled up and I would explode. I realized I was a person I didn't like. I would hold everything in, and before I knew it, I was full-blown yelling and reacting. I hated this version of myself, and certain relationships triggered it more, even thrived off it. I would get so frustrated and find myself in toxic cycles of lashing out, then hating myself because it didn't feel good to be like that. I would think, *Why are you fighting with me? Why are you doing this? Why are you making me like this?* While the other person didn't help, it was my actions that I was upset about and the one thing I was in control over. I stopped bottling things up. I worked on my communication skills, and when I had something to say, I would healthily say it. Instead of bottling up, I would voice something if it was bothering me, and doing this allowed the conversation to never get to the point where I was crying and begging for a fight to stop. I stopped engaging in this type of behavior and wouldn't match anyone's negative energy. I changed my actions with this toxic dynamic, and those unhealthy relationships faded out.

The old saying "actions speak louder than words," or my generation's new one "if they wanted to, they would," was something that I started to solely focus on. I started holding the people around me accountable when actions didn't line up. I went inward and held myself accountable as well, and I started small. If I said I was going to go food shopping after work, I made sure I did it. If I said I wasn't going to get drunk and text my ex over the weekend, I made sure that I didn't do it! This new awareness I had surrounding accountability and holding myself to these standards was another step to being my true and authentic self. And with this, I stopped surrounding myself with people and situations who weren't doing the same.

LET'S CHECK IN

I take this approach in all of my relationships now—with family, friendships, and romantic relationships. I pay attention to how much I am sacrificing myself and my peace for someone else. I realize that I am now truly surrounded by people who are authentic, where we respect each other's boundaries, who communicate, and who meet each other halfway.

Is there a relationship you can think of where you are not happy with the dynamic?

Make a list of actions only you can control to move out of this current cycle.

therapy

During this time, I found a therapist I clicked with and could trust to guide me through the extra layers of what I was experiencing. There are so many different styles of therapy out there, and I found myself getting discouraged a lot of the time when trying to find a clinician. It is imperative to find a therapist you feel comfortable with. I had given up a few times, and I heard from others that they "couldn't find someone they like" and I could totally relate! But like anything else, do not give up because the right fit is out there for everyone. My current therapist really guided me and taught me how to set real boundaries for myself for the first time at the age of thirty. Every time I would have a breakthrough in therapy, I would say to my therapist, "Okay, great, now what do I do to fix it?"

She would kind of laugh at me and say, "Sit in it and acknowledge it. Everything doesn't have a quick fix. Be aware of it, and see what comes up now that you know this about yourself."

This was hard for someone who has OCD tendencies and needs to plan every aspect of life. I had to let go of my need to control or the idea that a quick fix would make me feel better and make any issues I had go away. I started by putting myself first. If something didn't feel right for me, even if I didn't have a solid reason other than my body turning me one way over the other, I trusted it. I trusted and valued myself and my feelings. I stopped feeling the need to constantly explain myself. If I wanted to stay in on a weekend, I stayed in and didn't make up a story or validate it in any way. I would check in with myself every time I was saying yes or no to something and see where it was coming from. Was I doing this out of obligation or because it's something that's bringing me happiness? Was I eating (or not eating, in fact) to fill an emotional void, or was I fueling my body in a healthy way? Even my relationship with alcohol changed. I would still drink alcohol, as I do enjoy the taste of a good red wine or a dirty martini, but I would check in with myself to make sure I knew where it was coming from first. Am I drinking to mask and not feel what I'm feeling to take the edge off a stressful situation? Or am I sitting by the fire watching a movie or out to dinner and genuinely enjoying a glass of wine? Am I having sex with someone because it is coming from a place of being fun, intimate, and enjoyable? Or am I doing it to try to feel good about myself? I truly don't think there is anything wrong with casual sex and that sex in general is a natural part of life, but there were many times where I found myself doing it for validation, out of obligation, loneliness, or feeling like it defined me. I also stopped taking anything that wasn't prescribed to me or controlled by a doctor.

Have you ever received a text and once you see the name pop up on your phone, your body automatically reacts? You start smiling for no reason. Or maybe you automatically feel drained and have a huge pit in your stomach, all before you even communicate with that person! Pay close attention to these moments. Realize who and what is bringing out these physical reactions to you. Our body literally speaks to us, and once you start tuning into that part, it can be very difficult to ignore. I started to check in with myself constantly. It started daily, then turned into every time I was making a decision. I was closely paying attention to my body and would dissect why I was doing things. I called it the DIG Deep Method. Acronyms really were the only way for me to remember anything in school so I started making them for myself.

Deserve? Do I deserve this? Is it aligning with my worth and my values?

Intuition? What is my body telling me? How am I physically feeling when I am thinking about this? Is it screaming "Hell, yes!" or "Hell, frigging no!"

Goal? Does this support where I want to be in life? Is it bringing me closer to the life that I want?

I use this method for the biggest and smallest decisions.

For example:

Tony cheats on me and wants me to give him a second chance.

DIG:

Did I deserve for that to happen? Absolutely not.

What does your intuition tell you? He will do it to me again and I will never trust him.

Is this the type of life/relationship I want? No, it is not.

A friend wants to set you up with a great guy they work with.

DIG:

Does he have qualities that line up with my core values? Yes.

How does it make you feel? Nervous and pessimistic but also excited.

Is this the type of person you could maybe see yourself with? Yes, from the qualities that I know.

A guy texts you at 2 a.m. with, "WYD?"

DIG

Do I deserve to only be texted at 2 a.m.? No.

How does it feel in your body? Annoyed, frustrated, and used.

Is this the type of guy you want for your future? No, it is not.

All of these examples are relationship based, but I use them in every aspect of my life. I use it when I decide what to eat, when I want to drink, if I'm making a purchase, if I find myself angry or irritable, if I'm invited somewhere and I'm on the fence about going, or if I find myself in a situation that brings up anxiety. I use these tools to come back to my body, to pay attention to how I am physically feeling, and to identify where my true feelings or behavior is coming from.

LET'S CHECK IN

How can you do this too? Use the DIG Deep Method next time you are making a decision.

Write down what you realize and if it affects your original thought.

Deserve

Intuition

Goal

manifesting and gratitude

Journaling became a significant part of my therapy. It was a way for me to release the chatter that was going on in my head, which at that time, was consuming me. Stefani journaled often, and she recommended that I start with five things I was grateful for and five things I wanted to manifest, followed by a little paragraph of what I've been doing or whatever else came up for me. Most of my entries looked like this:

I am grateful for:

1. Jessica
2. My air conditioning
3. The health of my family
4. My friends
5. My apartment and independence

1. I will have the life that I want and feel I deserve.
2. I will be financially stable.
3. I will be loved by being my authentic self.
4. I will trust the path that I am on.
5. I will have faith that everything is going to work out.

Practicing gratitude daily became extremely grounding for me. It centered me and brought me balance. Focusing on what I had, especially things I would easily take for granted, would set the tone for the whole day. It automatically shifted my mindset into positivity. Even if I was having the worst day, the simple switch of putting my energy toward things that I did have, removed the energy and focus away from the things that I didn't.

When it came to manifesting, I leaned into my faith and my goals. I pictured what I wanted, how I wanted to feel, where I wanted to be, and pictured that I was already there. I pictured myself healed, I pictured myself okay being alone, and I pictured everything working out. I would speak these things to myself on a daily basis with confidence, which removed any of my stress and worry of how I would get there. I claimed it as if it was already mine and led every day with actions that aligned with the life I wanted—and eventually, it was mine.

After being with Jay, I was able to reflect on my relationship with Tony in certain ways I never saw before.

Both relationships had toxic aspects, but in very different ways. It gave me something to compare Tony and my relationship to, and I had never had that before. I was at my cousin Jenna's house one day for a barbeque. She's the oldest out of all of us and had 16-year-old triplets at the time. I loved being around them even though they made me feel very old! They would ask me to drive them everywhere or ask me to pick them and their friends up if they were stranded at the mall or a football game. I loved that they actually enjoyed being with me, and I wanted to set a good example for them. I was their age when I had met Tony and that was wild to me since they were the first babies I had been around and now they were these little adults. Anyway, I had been drinking the entire day in Jenna's yard. I wasn't drinking every single night anymore, but on the weekends, it was still a normal occurrence. One of the girls was talking about a boy she was seeing and asked the group if we thought people could change. I don't know if it was the alcohol, the sun or what, but I began to cry. This question triggered me so much. I was still constantly second-guessing myself—if I would have handled things differently or if I would have been in a better place in my life and if Tony could have changed, maybe we'd still be together. Maybe I would have been pregnant by now like we had always talked about. (In both of our houses, we had our kid's room planned out and would refer to it as "Gino's room.") Emma was living out the life that I had planned for myself, and I couldn't log onto Instagram without seeing a new couple I went to high school with announcing their wedding or pregnancy. Embarrassed by my emotional reaction, I felt like a drunk idiot crying in front of my family, especially my cousins, who I wanted nothing more than to be looked up to by them.

That night, Emma and Dom drove me home like they always did from Jenna's barbecues. I went home full of sadness, shame, and regret—wishing I could feel normal again. Of course, everyone else said it wasn't that big of a deal, but to me, it was. I was angry that Tony still had this effect on me and that with one small comment, I could be triggered so easily no matter how far I thought I had come. I felt like I was making progress with my healing. I was journaling a lot, in therapy, and was starting to meditate. I was slowly feeling better, so I thought. That's the thing about healing and working on yourself, it isn't always linear. You can think you're doing great and feel balanced, then one thing can happen and fuck it all up. Through my healing journey, I learned this was bound to happen, but the healing came from how I reacted to it.

Was I going to let this onslaught of emotions bring me right back into all of my old patterns and drink even more when I got home and invite a guy over to make myself temporarily feel better? Or was I going to reflect and see what I could do for it not to happen again? I spoke to my therapist about it that week and explained to her what had happened and how after all of this time I hated that I was still so consumed with the "what ifs" in my life.

"What would you want him to know?" my therapist asked.

"Just that I know all of the positives and good from our relationship and how everything happened so fast. I know there was real love there, and if he really did put the work in and wanted to try to rebuild any tiny bit that was left that I would have been willing to try to."

"Did you ever tell him that?"

"No, but he knows me, and he knows I would."

"If you never said it, he doesn't know."

She had suggested that I write to him and let him know how I was feeling.

After all this time? I thought. *Sounds so ridiculous, I am going to look like a wackjob!*

We still texted here and there, holidays and birthdays or random small check-ins, which definitely contributed to me feeling confused and still "attached" in a way. It would leave me with mixed messages as he would say things about still having regrets, but he still wasn't doing anything about it. I took three days to write a text and send it to him.

> Hey, I've been thinking a lot about some of the things you have said over the last few years, and it is confusing to me. I guess while I realize I have always felt that I've insinuated it, I never just said straight out that obviously if you were alone and on your own and wanted to try to even attempt to repair anything or start over and really put the work in, that I would be willing to do the work on my end too. I feel like you do know this already and you don't have to respond. This isn't a convo to have over text, but I just felt the need to say it straight out to you. Like I always have said, I just want you to be happy.

I think I tossed my phone across the room face down after I sent it and didn't look at it for the rest of the day. I started running around with sage like a desperate person instead. Even after sending it, I sensed a weight lifted from me. I couldn't explain it. It didn't even matter what his answer was, but I had truly said what was on my mind after all of this time, and by saying it straight out, no games, no ego, and no assuming what he already knew or didn't know, it was released from me.

He had responded a day or so later with an equally thought-out text. It wasn't an easy text to read, for many reasons. It was hard to go back and hear his vulnerability after all of this time, but it also was exactly what I needed to truly be able to move on from him and our life together. He gave me a clear answer. No matter what his response was, I had the closure I needed. I said what I had to say. I no longer had the "what ifs." I had given him a real opportunity, and he responded to it. He could no longer send me mixed messages because he just gave me the reality, straight out, loud and clear. I never questioned it again because despite his actions over the months and the back and forth, this was the reality, and I finally accepted it.

I've reflected on this moment, on how maybe if I would have said these things earlier to him, I would have healed faster. But the truth is, I sent the message at the perfect time and finally felt free of him and our relationship without any questions or regrets. From then on, any communication between us stopped.

LET'S CHECK IN

I've written so many letters in general—to myself, to my future self, to Tony, to the twenty-something-year-old gym girl—and it has been so cleansing. Many times, after I write a letter, I release it from my body, meditate, burn the letter, and let it go. It is beyond healing. It has allowed me to let go of focusing on any negative energy, to let it go if I felt something weighing on me.

- Who do you need to write to in your life today?
- What emotions are you carrying that are ready to be released?
- Is there somewhere in your life where you are feeling stuck or need to get out?
- When you're ready, write that letter.

For me, I knew I needed him to see it. You'll know if that is the case for you, too; and if not, the practice of writing will help in releasing what you're holding onto.

Are you ready? Who are you writing to and why? Give it a go, babe.

yoga

You know those girls who go through a breakup and throw themselves into the gym and end up looking better than ever? Yeah, that wasn't me. I never found joy from working out. I would like how I felt afterward or when I would see results in my body physically, but I sincerely loathed the whole process. I would work in the city all day, change in the bathroom, race to the bus to get to a workout class and would literally be staring at the clock the entire time waiting for it to be over. There was nothing about it that made me happy. I would be so cranky the whole way home from work, praying that I would hit traffic so I would miss the very expensive, non-refundable class I had already paid for. I do think it is very important to move your body, but you need to find a way that makes you happy while doing so.

Throughout my divorce and newly single life, I found the "Yoga with Adriene" channel on YouTube. I always liked the idea of yoga, but I had this misconception that in order to do it I had to be a vegan who knew how to stand on my head and turn my body into a pretzel. I was the furthest thing from that; I could barely touch my toes. I think the reason this class stood out to me was that she had a twenty-two-minute video called "Yoga for a Hangover." *Was this made for me?*

I instantly connected with her and the community she had built. There were videos anywhere from ten-minute meditations to forty-minute core workouts. I swear, she has a yoga class for everything: Yoga for Heartbreak, Yoga for Anxiety, Yoga for Clarity, Yoga for Nighttime—you name it, and there's a video for it. There was an instant relatability to what she was teaching, even though it was through my living room TV (and even with Jess jumping on me the whole time I was down on the floor). I found myself pausing the video and Googling terms that she was using because I wanted to understand it more. I hated school and never found myself good at a subject that I wasn't genuinely interested in. One night, I started Googling "Learn about yoga" and "Yoga schools" and found there were places to study it and become a certified yoga instructor. This was the last thing I wanted to do or be. It was not my goal to stand up and teach a class, and the thought sprung into my mind of *Who the hell would want to learn anything from me?* But I was intrigued.

It just so happened that week I had received a surprise bonus from work that was neither common nor expected. The universe really does work in your favor when you surrender to it and start trusting it. I felt it was meant to go toward something positive in my life, other than a few bottles of Grey Goose and red wine. I ended up making some calls the next day, used my bonus money, and signed up for a five-month Yoga Teacher Training course.

Immediately, impostor syndrome set in. I had been doing basic yoga for a few months in my one-bedroom apartment and now I was going to a full-blown course on it?! *Who the F did I think I was?* But I already had committed to it. I was doing it for my brain and for something positive to put my energy toward. I hoped I would learn something new in the process, and let me tell you, I learned more than I could ever have imagined. Not so much physically but more about the history of yoga, and most importantly, I discovered a lot about myself.

The class was every Sunday in New Jersey about a half hour away from me. I was nervous but also excited. The moment I entered the class, I knew I had made the right decision. It was filled with women and men of all different ages and different backgrounds and interests. We sat in a circle on our yoga mats and had to say what brought us here. I kept it vague: "I am a beginner, and I want to understand the history and all the terms of yoga so I can keep up better in class."

I felt silly as I said it out loud. It sounded so lame next to everyone who had dedicated most of their lives and careers to this very moment, but as I looked up, I was surrounded by nodding and accepting people. We received a whole course load of work and assignments. I loved having homework and things to read every week and couldn't wait for Sunday to come so I could go back to the studio for the day and learn more. I felt like I had a purpose again. I wasn't going out on Saturday nights and drinking the night away since I had to get up early on Sundays. I stopped drinking just to drink because I was getting my out-of-studio hours in on my free time and reading myself to sleep.

Meditation was a large part of our coursework as well, and I started doing it more than ever. I would find a guided meditation on YouTube and do it for ten minutes at a time on my commute to and from work every day. I then started doing it on my own time, at night before bed or in the middle of the day if I was stressed, and in the morning on weekends. It was life changing for me and still is to this day.

One of our assignments was to read Deepak Chopra's book, *The Seven Spiritual Laws of Success*. My yoga teacher actually studied with him early in her career and passed on so many of his teachings to us. This book, too, is something that changed my life. I still randomly open it up and read one of his laws when I feel off balance, or when I have to get grounded and center myself. The biggest law that stood out for me was "The Law of Non-Judgment." I became so present and mindful about every time I was judging someone, especially myself. I would catch myself and try to figure out where it came from. The internal negative dialogue began to fade, and eventually, the negativity became much quieter. Don't get me wrong, it is still there, but it is nowhere near as mean, and I am aware of it now.

Awareness is such a monumental step to anything you want to do or change. There are times I put on my jeans and say, "Ugh, you shouldn't have had that pizza last night!" But I bounce back from it quickly and respond with, "Okay, well you did enjoy the pizza, right?! Did it make you happy?" or "Good for you, you're allowed, and your jeans being tight does not define you as a person." I have conversations with myself like this on a daily basis.

It was like once I made the conscious decision to shift my mindset and tell myself I didn't like the road I was going down, everything changed for me. I realized how different everyone's path was. I was so empowered, feeling like I could be spiritual while still dropping the F-bomb and eating filet mignon when I wanted to. I found something that I wouldn't normally have done and was able to remain my true self in the process. It made me realize that you don't have to have society's version of what a career, a relationship, or a hobby should look like. If your ideal weekend and idea of "winding down" is backpacking in the woods and sleeping in a tent, you can still have similar interests and a bond with someone who would rather go to a spa and sleep on white bedding.

I also think it is so important to own it, whatever it is! It doesn't have to make you a "hippie" or "bougie." Whatever brings you joy on the inside is what you should do. I am different from a lot of my friends; they all know me as someone who likes to stay home and who is in bed by 8:00 p.m. if I have work the next day, and they love me for it. My family knows that I spend my Sundays food shopping and mentally preparing for the week. They don't try to change me, and they don't judge me for being different from them.

I don't know if it is because I started to exude this "unapologetically myself" energy, but I would only surround myself with people who accepted me and embraced exactly who I was. It took a while for me to get to this point; it was such a journey. I grew up wanting everyone to like me, and to make others' lives easier at the expense of my own life, especially in my romantic relationships. I didn't value my emotions or feelings enough to put them first, and at the end of the day, these were the ones I should have been prioritizing all along.

The six months of yoga school really flew by, and I felt so accomplished. I felt good about myself for the first time in a really long time. I was at a point where I trusted myself and felt that I and my feelings were valid and important. I felt worthy! Both of my sisters came to my "graduation" along with my new niece, and I was very emotional in a good way. I was now certified in yoga and meditation and felt like I had such a clear and new vision of life to move forward with. And no, I still couldn't stand on my head or turn my body into a pretzel!

LET'S CHECK IN

What is your favorite way to move your body?

As you heal, you may want to try something new. I can't stress enough how amazing it is to say yes to the things that intimidate or scare you.

Is there something right now that you would love to try?

Write it down and look up where you could take a class or join a group to further your learning and experience about the things you're passionate about.

signs

I went from feeling disposable and unworthy to realizing how valuable I was, and I stepped into that version of myself daily. Trust me, babe, you will get there too! It took a lot of time, but before I knew it, I was comfortable and happy living on my own. I loved my apartment, but I started to have some water issues. Every time it would rain, I would end up getting flooded. I was purchasing multiple sump pumps and hired different plumbers who had no solution. My original landlord had sold the house, and I was so sad because I really liked him. The new landlords were very nice except for the strain in communication, especially when it came to the flooding. I was going through far too many area rugs and knew it was time to start looking for better accommodations.

The thought of moving again brought up a fair amount of anxiety. Every time I had moved in the past, it was usually for a negative reason. The first was in my youth when my parents were in over their heads and we couldn't afford our house anymore. The last time, as you know, was moving out of the house Tony and I had created a whole life around. I do wish I had video footage of me attempting to parallel park the U-Haul on my own, though. Talk about comic relief!

Instead of holding on to the anxiety, I decided to take action. I texted my old landlord and asked him to keep me in mind if he heard of any apartments becoming available. To my delight, he replied right away saying that his mother had an available apartment, brand new, right down the block and for the same price I was paying. *Thank you, universe!* It was totally meant to be. Even though I was excited, I also knew moving again would trigger inner wounds. I was scared to make the jump because I had a lot of fear surrounding the unknown. I made endless pros and cons lists between the two apartments.

Pros

- New construction
- Same area
- No water issues
- Landlord

Cons

- Love my current neighbors
- No designated parking spot
- Would have to drive to the bus stop
- Kitchen table won't fit
- Train is loud when it goes by

I had to let them know if I wanted the apartment that week and also give my current landlord thirty-days' notice. Of course, I didn't have any water issues for the two weeks this internal spiral was going on. *Maybe it is fixed, and I should just stay in what's familiar and safe*, I thought. On the morning I had to make my decision, my first thought was to ask for a sign. It sounded more like "Ugh, please let something happen today to help me make my decision: move or don't move."

I did this a lot since that day sitting in the church in London. I relied on my faith and truly believed I would always be guided. I peeled myself out of bed and went straight to the bathroom to brush my teeth. I was finishing up and was leaning into the sink to make my final rinse, when I heard a gurgling coming from down the drain. I stood up away from it and black water started slowly coming up the drain; it filled up the sink, then went back down the drain. That was the end of the noise; I felt like I had imagined it. I was there for two years and not one of the issues I had ever experienced was ever in the bathroom, let alone in the sink. My decision was made. I always say, "If it feels like a sign to you, then it is a sign," but this was one of the clearest, loudest, and grossest signs I have ever received.

After that, I knew I could change the narrative surrounding my triggers about moving and make this one an exciting experience. Yes, I was having issues, so I did feel like I had to move, but it was on my terms for the first time, and it was me wanting to and not being forced to. The minute I let go and decided it was going to be a positive experience, it was. Jess and I were on the move again! My aunt and Emma helped me unpack all day, and my brother Danny hung up all of my pictures and curtains. He put together some shelves for my closet, and I picked all new paint colors. The furniture I had picked out and purchased myself over the last two years worked well in the new space.

My first night was the total opposite of my first night in my last place. Justin, Frank, Nicole, and my new friends Collette and TJ came over with all different kinds of pizzas and bottles of wine. We spent the night cleaning, unpacking, and sitting on the floor in the living room eating and laughing. It was the perfect first memory for this new chapter of my life. I remember looking around at the new space and my new friends with such gratitude. Everything that had happened in my life had brought me to this very moment, and I was feeling genuinely at peace. I realized that as much as I loved my last apartment, and the occasional great memory I had there, the majority of them were sad and dark. I was drunk or high 75 percent of the nights spent there over the two years. I think I can safely say that I cried at least once every day. It was the place I hit rock bottom. It was time for a new chapter, a new beginning. I was getting to know my authentic self, and I was trusting myself for the first time in my life. I knew this was the right move for me.

Journal entry—October 2019

I truly believe that everything is going to work out, and a lot of my doubts in general have become less and less. Not for any reason specifically, but I really have learned to try and pay attention to my gut when it comes to making any decisions. I am preparing to move into my new apartment, and I am feeling scared of not making the right decision—but also so excited. This is the first time I am moving somewhere that I really like and because I want to, not because I have to.

It is a newer place, and I know this is the right move for me. I love the energy there! I feel like there are a lot of sad memories in my current apartment.

I do always still pray and hope that I am making the right decisions, but I trust myself so much more than I ever did. I have such an amazing and close group of SOLID friends right now, and this is the first time in my life I can really say that. I am also closer than ever with my cousins, and it is a really great feeling having them around. I feel so supported. We are all making so many amazing memories. I can't help but realize that all of these relationships (with Stefani, Nicole, Justin, Lana, Jenna, and Fran) that I have now, I probably wouldn't have had if I had stayed on the path that I had originally planned in life. It's so bizarre how that can feel like a lifetime ago, yet I could easily close my eyes and picture myself back in my old life and my old house. Now though, I can think about it and it brings me a nostalgic feeling opposed to the pain and confusion it used to. I really do have such a different and strong relationship with myself. I have been working so hard on that. I want to continue to grow and build that. I truly believe everything will work out, and I can't wait for the new beginnings that will come with this apartment.

The day did come when I made peace with my divorce and my life with Tony ending and focused on the lessons it had taught me. I seriously thought this feeling would never come! I was slowly coming down from the roller coaster of the Jay situation and started to feel free, grounded, and clear. I loved my new apartment. I felt lonely at times, but I felt stronger too. For the first time, I knew who I was deep down and what I wanted out of my life. With Tony and Jay, I was in the same position where my heart wanted one thing, but my instinct was telling me something totally different, and it felt right. I was leading with my intuition and instinct more than ever. There I was, in my new space—alone again. No friendly neighbors, no Tony, no dating apps, no Jay, no excessive drinking, no settling, no meaningless hookups, just *me*. And even though it was uncomfortable, I knew it was exactly where I needed to be.

I was no longer chasing plans. On my way home from work one evening I received a call from a friend asking me to go for drinks. I was drained and exhausted from the work week and told her I wasn't up for it. As I walked into my empty apartment instead and sat down on my couch with a big cup of tea, I looked around and realized how genuinely happy I was to be home. I realized that I didn't have to chase plans anymore and go out just to go out. I wasn't scrolling through my phone for a guy to

CASSANDRA DECICCO

text to come over just so I wasn't alone. Not only was I okay being home alone with myself, my thoughts, and my reality, I was happy about it. This was a significant turning point for me.

By embracing my alone time, I let go of the "when I meet someone" mentality I had drilled inside of myself and continued to take control of my life. I traveled, I cooked only when I wanted to, I learned how to do things around my apartment (with the thanks of YouTube, lol), and felt proud of myself for the first time because I was genuinely okay. I no longer felt like I needed to find a guy to complete me or my life.

LET'S CHECK IN

This was a big aha moment for me. Have you ever been in a situation where you thought you would never feel okay again, let alone happy?

During the darkest times (those two years), I never thought I could find the light, yet somehow, through a lot of tears and too many bottles of wine, I broke through. Even if it doesn't seem possible right now, take a moment and write this out:

One day, I'll break through these dark days, and when the light shines through I will feel . . .

Tuck this one away and come back to it every now and then. You will be amazed when this feeling happens.

pressure

It may sound super cliché, but instead of focusing all my time and effort into a dating profile or the perfect Instagram caption, I went inward and solely focused on doing the work on myself. I dove into therapy even more and dug deep. I began dealing with all of my shit that I had buried over my thirty-one years. No longer ignoring the questions that had been lurking within me, I opened up and started asking "why?"

Why am I *so* insecure?

Why do I accept unacceptable behavior?

Why do I avoid conflict and take on the caretaker role?

Why do I feel others' feelings and needs are more important than my own?

Why do I feel *so* unworthy?

These were difficult questions to ask, but I knew they had to be addressed. Leaning into my faith and letting go helped me to understand that all I could control at that moment was to become the best version of myself. If someone came into my life who could add value and had also done the work on their end, then he's the guy I wanted to be with. It wasn't always easy to stay in this mindset, however. I struggled with feelings of judgment by those around me. "Are you dating anyone?" was often the first question anyone asked when having a conversation. Despite feeling more myself and mentally healthier than ever, society only wanted to know who I was dating. I have countless memories of birthdays and Christmases receiving texts like "Did you get the ring yet?" As much as I was secure and happy with the timeline Tony and I were on, it would always put a cloud over the day getting asked these questions. I felt like I had to defend why we weren't engaged yet. I can imagine it is the same when a couple gets married, society wants to know when they are having kids or why they haven't had kids yet. It is so frustrating. It makes me so upset/triggered when I hear someone judging or questioning another person or another couple's timeline. It's unfair. Everyone should be able to live life on their terms and not based on what society "expects" of you.

I knew I wasn't the only person who felt this way, at least, I hoped. One summer day, around this time, I ran into an old friend on my lunch break. We were talking on a corner while quickly catching up when I asked how her boyfriend was doing. Her energy kind of shut down as she immediately said, "Good, we're not engaged yet, but—" and started to explain everything else they had going on as a couple.

I felt so sad for her that despite all of the milestones she and her boyfriend had hit as a couple, she felt the need to stand there explaining to me why she wasn't engaged yet. I could tell she was feeling pressured from people around her and that it was weighing on her, even though she was secure and happy with where they were. I cut her off and said just that; to stop defending why she wasn't engaged yet and embrace where she was. There are people who think that getting engaged and getting married are the finish line in life and project it onto everyone they meet when that's not the case for everyone. After I shared that with her, her whole energy changed and she went from being almost defensive to relieved. She thanked me as we continued to talk about all of the positives she had going on, and we had a great conversation.

To me:

- If I was dating someone and I was happy and excited about it and wanted to talk about it, I would bring it up.
- If a couple is at the point when they are ready to be engaged, they will be engaged and will be celebrating it.
- If a couple wants a baby and they aren't pregnant yet, I am sure they are doing everything they can to make it happen and will talk about it when they are ready.

I had accepted being single and had stopped trying to explain myself every time someone asked me, "Still no guy?"

I owned it. I would put a big smile on my face and just say, "Nope!" It truly just wasn't my time. If Mr. Right had come falling through my ceiling into the middle of my living room at that time, I would have screwed it up in a second because of the spiral of new emotions I was dealing with. I was healing, I was doing inner child work, and I was learning so much about myself that deep down, I knew instead of finding the one, I had to let go and trust the timing of my life. I knew I would meet someone eventually, but it just wasn't high on my list. I know when I click with someone, and I know when I don't—and that's okay. I told my friends and family over and over, "When I meet the one, trust me I will know right off the bat and scream it from the rooftops, and you will be the first to know."

I can confidently say that when I do meet someone and decide to pursue a relationship, it is going to be coming from a place of love and not loneliness. Some days, I wish I could go back to my insecure and younger self, shake that girl, and tell her, "Let go of any idea you have to find someone else to complete you. Let go of all the *shoulds* from society or the people around you. Do things that make you feel complete and fulfilled on your own. That way, if the right person comes along, they can add to your happiness. You do not need anyone to come and save you—you have it within yourself. You are enough on your own, and don't let anyone tell you anything different. Do not settle! Not for the job, not for the guy on Bumble, not for anything less that you truly feel deep down in your gut is the right thing. Know your values and let go of anything or anyone that does not align with them. I encourage you to reflect on your values and what you want for your life. Think about them hard and write them down. Make a long list and read it back to yourself weekly. Check in with yourself and the life you are living and make sure you are making choices that are going toward the life that you want."

I gave myself permission to take a sabbatical from dating and the pressures surrounding it. In the past, I was quick to mask the loneliness despite how it made me feel instead of sitting in the uncomfortableness and learning how to be okay with it. I realized it was okay to be happy and independent, while still having loneliness creep in at times and not jump to mask that feeling with people or situations that did not bring out the best of me or my authentic self. Don't get me wrong, I still did want love again, it just wasn't my main priority. The main relationship I was focusing on was the one I had with myself. There were plenty of times I would feel lonely and think how certain things may have been "more fun" with a partner, but overall, I was genuinely happy in the life I had created all on my own. Being able to sit on the couch in my underwear whenever I wanted and eat Nutella out of the jar was definitely a bonus!

LET'S CHECK IN

Do you feel pressure from others regarding an area in your life?

I know it may sound impossible, but I'm going to encourage you to do something. Make a list of five things that are a bonus of the life you are living.

- What do you love about your time?
- What is sweet about the time you have right now?

If your list is longer, then keep writing! Not only will this reframe the judgments you may be battling with, but it will also create a mind frame that allows you to value what you have with yourself right now.

2020

Like for many others, 2020 was a life-changing year for me. It started with an amazing trip to Bali with my two good friends, only to come home to isolation, loss, grief, and fear of the unknown. This resulted in another journey involving questioning of my newfound faith for the first time. The year began with a rough peak season at work where I was feeling very drained, underpaid, and unappreciated. It was the only part of my life where I felt I was not following my authentic self, but hey, what was I going to do? I had a secure job that I was good at, and like many, I felt like it was the only way. Because of my three-hour commute to and from NYC every day, I had absolutely no work-life balance. From Monday to Friday,

I would end up useless once I got home, jumping right in the shower and getting into bed. My Saturdays were spent running errands and spending time with my niece when I could, and Sundays I would do laundry while cleaning my apartment and planning meals and my hair-washing schedule for the week. I had been in this cycle for years, and it was taking a toll on my overall happiness.

Even though I love being home more than anything else, I really enjoy traveling also. I am obsessed with seeing new places and getting away from the hustle and the busy life that comes from living in New York. I never really went away to "party" but more to wind down and disconnect from everyday life. I traveled more after my divorce than I ever had in my whole life. Growing up, I went away with my family every summer, but as we got older and money got tighter, we did day trips instead. Tony and I had only gone away a handful of times throughout our relationship. In fact, our honeymoon was the first and only time we were on a plane together. Since becoming single, I have been to Nevada, Nashville, Florida, California (for my thirtieth birthday), glamping upstate in the Finger Lakes, weekends in the Hamptons, tubing in the Catskills, and yearly trips to Binghamton and Pennsylvania with my family. But my favorite trip of all was to Bali!

My good friend Fran was someone with whom I did

a lot of the that traveling. She was such a grounded and balanced free-spirit, and I frequently looked up to her. I had met her when I was about eighteen, and we'd clicked right away. She moved to the city, became a yoga teacher, and would travel all over the world—solo! I would watch her Instagram stories and live vicariously through her for so many years with a lot of admiration. We stayed close and eventually became each other's travel buddy. No matter where we were, we would find ourselves laughing until our stomachs hurt one minute, then in deep conversation about life the next. I told Stefani about our plans for Bali, and she lit up like a Christmas tree. She knew Fran from over the years as well, and this was going to be our first trip together.

A few weeks and a twenty-four-hour plane ride later, we arrived in Bali. Our plane was empty on the way due to the beginning of the COVID-19 virus coming to the United States. To be honest, at that time, it was something we knew was an issue in China but did not think it would ever become as global and fatal as it turned out to be. We arrived at our villa about 9 p.m. Bali time, in awe of how beautiful it was. We were all extremely jet-lagged and sat up until 4 a.m. bonding in our outdoor living room that had the cutest tiniest lizards crawling everywhere. I had bought us all travel journals to remember our trip, and I think that was the only night we actually wrote in them, but we lay in bed answering the questions the journal asked together. The first page said:

I dedicate this journey to: *myself, the person I want to be.*

What are your hopes for this trip? *I hope to find peace with where I am at in my life.*

As much as I had started my spiritual journey, I was nowhere near where I wanted to be. I still had doubts about the future, wondered if I'd made the right choices in life in general, and whether I was going to be alone forever. I would get worried that if I did start to become overly content and happy on my own that it would take someone impossibly unrealistic for me to entertain being with them because I didn't want to screw up the little bubble of peace that I had created. I was feeling drained and unfulfilled from my nine-to-five job, the commute each way was killing me, and I felt very lost and disconnected from myself and my faith. One of the main things I would pray for was clarity and a clear and pure reassurance that I was on the right path and that everything would be okay.

We spent our time in Bali going on day trips to beaches and temples, shopping the streets of Ubud, and hiking up Mt. Batur at 3 a.m. for the sunrise. We would get the best foot massages I've ever had for eight dollars every day and ride scooters through the streets for hours without a care in the world. It was absolute bliss. It seriously felt like another world.

The two weeks we were in Bali, COVID-19 started exploding in New York City. We kept in touch with our families and friends, but it really did seem like it shut down overnight. We arrived back in New York on March 21, and the US closed its borders the very next day. We made it home just in time, having no idea what we were coming home to. It was a very unknown and sad time for many people. My heart broke watching the news, hearing the numbers rising every day and the stories about everyone losing loved ones, and even worse, not being able to be with them when they did. I felt so sad for all of the business owners who were unable to survive through this. Hugs became something that were danger-ous. (Physical touch is my love language, remember, I'm a BIG hugger!) Relationships were now mostly through FaceTime. I lived alone and missed my family so much, specifically my Nanny who was ninety years old and prone to pneumonia, so definitely considered high-risk. She lived with my aunt in New Jersey at this point, and we arranged for an outdoor social-distanced visit once the weather started getting nicer, which became the new normal for a while.

I never thought that the day would come where I actually liked being alone. The misconception that alone meant lonely was just not the case. I started to fully embrace it. Despite the sadness that was going on in the world and this wild way we were all now living, I did realize a lot about myself. I enjoyed slowing down, I loved not running around constantly and especially not commuting to work every day. I actually found myself way more productive with work because I wasn't so burned out from the daily commute. I realized I did like my job and what I did every day, but I did not like traveling and the lack of work-life balance that went along with it. I found a new routine, and I was completely in love with it. I spent so much more time with Jess, who was used to being alone for twelve hours a day. Running errands and organizing my apartment became much easier and more enjoyable. I continued therapy on a weekly basis via Zoom and had a whole morning routine of meditating, writing, and doing yoga during the time I would have been sitting in traffic on the express bus. I felt so recharged and so much more like myself. I honestly loved everything about it and never wanted to go back to the office.

LET'S CHECK IN

See if you can point out parts of your life that drain you and parts that fill you up! Make a list and really tune into how what you do every day makes you feel.

Is there anything on the side that drains you that you can do something to lessen it, or even better, cut it completely out?

Look at the list of positives and be aware of increasing the time you spend on them. See my list below:

Top 5 things that drain me

Commuting to the city

Gossip & negative talk

Confrontation

Caring about what others think

Online dating

Top 5 things that fill me up

Going to sleep early

Spending time with my nieces

Meditation & journaling every day

Spending time with Emma and my friends

Laughing

loss

I wish when I was going through these stages of my journey that I knew it wasn't just one straight road to being healed. I could have a week of feeling so strong and positive for the future to completely questioning my faith and wondering if it all really was going to work out in the end. It was—and still is—such an up and down process. I used to resist the lows because I felt as if I was failing. Now I see that we're always going to be faced with lows in our lives, but it is how we handle ourselves in these moments that show the real growth and the real part of healing.

I was truly tested with this the last week of June when I had to make the difficult decision to put Jess down. I was a mess and completely devastated. My apartment was the emptiest it had ever been since I'd been there. I was so heartbroken. In the middle of a pandemic I was utterly alone, and it hit me hard. Having Jess was the one stable thing in my whole life; she honestly saved my life after my divorce. Jess was by my side for fifteen years and slept with me every single night, through all the ups and downs. I didn't know how I would ever get over the pain I felt from losing her. Having her and the unconditional love she showed me was the one and only thing that had been constant through my life, and now she was gone too. It was the hardest thing I had ever gone through.

Sadly, the very next week, my sweet Nanny passed away also. I thought I was numb from grief already, but I was able to feel even sadder than I ever thought possible. I went back into caretaker mode. I pushed my feelings aside and knew I had to be strong for my dad and my aunt. Emma, Kelsey, and I all rushed to New Jersey to be with them, and I spent the next week planning the funeral and writing her eulogy. I became obsessed with writing that last year.

Nanny was ninety. She lived an amazing life, and I knew this day would come eventually. The same with Jess. Regardless of the reality, I wasn't prepared to say any of these goodbyes. One of my main fears when Jess passed was worrying that she didn't know anyone in heaven. She was happiest when she was with me, and I felt like I couldn't protect her wherever she was. My faith was being tested again. I couldn't help but find peace in thinking she and Nanny were both together now, taking care of each other.

Even though I was living through a global pandemic, I was grateful that I was able to spend the last three months of Jess's life with her all day, every day. Moments like these reaffirm my belief that everything happens for a reason, even if we don't know what that is at the time. Following tragedy, hardship, and things that are out of our control, we can make a conscious effort to see some type of good in whatever the experience is for ourselves and learn, appreciate, or grow from it—and not fall apart.

I had made the decision to give myself permission to feel what I was feeling and to be sad about what I was going through. Unlike my divorce, when I put on a strong front and walked around like I was fine when I clearly wasn't, I decided not to bury this emotion of grief and just move through it. I told everyone and anyone who would listen about it— even to the delivery guy who brought me food! My friends all thought I was nuts for how much I talked about it, but it was what I was going through at the time, and I wasn't going to pretend it wasn't happening.

LET'S CHECK IN

I realized something had changed inside of me. I was growing and it felt really good. These were challenging times to say the least, but I didn't rely on my old patterns. I chose the ones I had been working on over the years leading up to these losses. It's worth the work.

Do you have an area in your life right now that needs an extra dose of faith?

It doesn't mean you won't feel the pain, but somehow, you will know that you won't be totally alone in the midst of it.

authenticity

As the dark clouds of grief were parting, I finally let go of worrying if other people liked me, and continued to focus on liking myself. Figuring out who your authentic self is can be a scary and intimidating process, especially for those who don't necessarily like themselves. I think self-love is a great goal to have, but it can be discouraging for some people. Love is experienced differently for everyone. Some have only been hurt by people they love, many have lost their worth in people they love, others have been programmed to feel that they are unlovable, and some have loved people or things that are toxic or unhealthy for them. It is possible that many will naturally equate love to something that ends up being disappointing or something that will hurt them. This is why my goal for myself was to chip away at my self-hate little by little. When I would find myself in the negative self-talk reel, I would become aware of it. I would ask myself where it was coming from and why I was feeling this way. I would ask myself if I would talk to anyone I cared about the way I was speaking to myself. Practicing this slowly turned into self-acceptance. I was able to get rid of the nasty, and at times vicious, dialogue going on in my head and stop it in its tracks. I would accept that it's okay to feel certain ways, but it doesn't define you, and it certainly does not warrant you speaking to yourself like you're a piece of shit.

Through self-acceptance, I was able to focus on things I did like about myself. I would pay close attention to what I was doing when I felt my best. I would ask myself who I was with, what I was doing, and what I was wearing. I would do those things more.

I had gained twenty-five pounds during the year of 2020 and definitely did not feel my best. My body image issues that I have always dealt with were high. The days of working from home and not racing around the city anymore, ordering food, and drinking wine every night started to catch up to me. Feeling depressed after losing Jess and Nanny and not going for my usual walks also changed my body. I had no energy and did not know the body that I was in. I was living in leggings because none of my jeans fit, and I would come home from running errands and rip my bra off because it was suffocating me. As much as I had accepted where it was coming from, I was still so down on myself because of how physically uncomfortable I was. I was talking to my therapist about it one day and she said, "Why don't you go buy a bigger bra and bigger jeans?"

"No! That would mean that I am intending on maintaining this weight and I'm not!" I snapped back.

"It is okay to change sizes and to gain weight, and it is a solution instead of you wearing clothes that don't fit you, that are making you uncomfortable, and having negative dialogue with yourself," she replied.

She was right. Why was I insisting on feeling like a schlep in clothes that didn't fit me? I ordered a new bra, some new jeans, and new underwear that night. The next week when I ran out to run errands, I put my jeans on that fit me great. I felt like an actual human being instead of hiding in my leggings and oversized thermals like I had been doing all year. I came home and didn't rip my bra off and throw on a huge t-shirt, because I was wearing one that fit me and that I was comfortable in. There was no negative self-talk while getting ready that morning.

Was I happy with where my body was? No, I was not. But I had accepted it because I was accepting what I had been through, and it was a huge step for me.

I was always looking to explore different outlets of therapy. I did traditional talk therapy weekly, inner child work, Reiki healing, and anything else I could find. During the pandemic, I took an online course from one of my favorite Instagram accounts, and it was life changing for me. It was filled with videos, meditations, and worksheets to take a deep dive look at yourself and learn how to become whole on your own. The exercise that resonated most for me was figuring out your core values and not compromising them when it comes to any relationships in your life. Don't get me wrong, of course you may meet someone who doesn't check all of your boxes, and I don't think that means to shut it down, but if someone is not aligning with your true values and what is most important to you, that will eventually lead to an unbalanced dynamic. Through this exercise I was able to come up with a list of values that were important to me, but I came to realize that my top five core values were:

1. Love and respect (they are equally important to me!)
2. Communication
3. Acceptance
4. Loyalty and honesty
5. Quality time

These are the five things I will not compromise on when it comes to being in a relationship moving forward. They are things that make me feel loved and safe in any relationship in my life. Something else I learned is that it is easy to fall into focusing on two strong core values without realizing it and compromising the rest. With Tony, I truly felt he loved and accepted me, but I compromised feeling respected and not having our one-on-one time together, which eventually blew up in our faces. It's important to know these values for yourself and keep them in mind. Start practicing them yourself.

So often we shift ourselves to fit another person's mold, just to have someone to be with, to feel complete. What happens, however, is we end up completely losing ourselves. I encourage you to unapologetically be yourself. Make sure that whatever you choose to do, it is coming from a place of want and love and adding to the amazing person you already are, not defining it. If you like to go to sleep at 8:30 p.m., own it. If you go out five nights a week, own it. As long as whatever you are doing is true to you and brings you joy—do it! Implement your values yourself, put yourself on that pedestal, and show up as that person every day. Know that you are worth it and start acting like it. Celebrate your little wins and make sure to give yourself the credit you deserve.

I've realized that when bad things happen to us, it gives

us the opportunity to get closer to our authentic self or move us farther away from it. It is so easy to lose yourself in anger or numb the pain when going through grief or any type of transition. It is much easier to mask these things instead of feeling what is really going on. However, these are the times that can also truly transform us.

I will never be the person I was again before my marriage ended. It was a big loss, a monumental shake-up for me, but I was able to grow from it. I was forced to look at myself and address what my true issues were within myself. I took control of my own happiness. I had to look at myself and couldn't blame anyone else for the mental state I was in. I became a better version of myself through it, a more self-aware version of myself who strived to do better. I realized I was enough on my own, more than enough, in fact.

LET'S CHECK IN

A question to ask yourself during days when you feel like going back to old patterns is "Do I want the version of me that rises above or do I want the version of me that gets stuck?"

It's a kick in the gut sometimes because the work is hard, but the reward in the rise is worth it every time.

Make a list of your top five values. How can you start incorporating these things into your everyday life?

comparison

I didn't date at all during the pandemic. Eventually the time came when all of my friends were now in relationships, all of whom I loved and became great friends with. Emma and Dom just had their second daughter (my second goddaughter), and I was filled with new and exciting love all around me, just not my own.

This period was a weird time for Emma and me. For our whole lives, we had always been on the same page with everything. We always joke that growing up as twin sisters, we only remember one fight we ever were in, which lasted only twenty-four hours. Even now, we weren't fighting, but we were on different pages in our lives. Emma was running her successful business from home, while Dom was also working in the next room all while having a spunky 3-year-old and a newborn. She was constantly on the go, constantly around people, and craved some quiet. Then there was me, who was constantly alone and isolated in an apartment where you could hear a pin drop. There were some days that went by when I would realize, *Wow, I haven't had any human interaction today.* Around this time, I had decided to book a consultation and start testing for the possibility of freezing my eggs. I was feeling the pressure of the "biological clock" creeping in. The early testing didn't give me the answers I was hoping for, which would have been: "Oh, you're only thirty-two, your eggs are great, and you have plenty of time to decide whether you want to do this and to financially prepare for this."

Unfortunately, the response I got was that my egg count was that of a 45-year-old, and I should freeze my eggs sooner than later. This was hard for me to wrap my head around. Another "plan" I had for my life that might not be a reality. Emma had two beautiful and healthy girls as a result of getting pregnant fairly easily. It would be difficult for us to not want to give each other the whole "must be nice" comment. She was stressed with her husband and kids while I was getting coffee and roaming around Target for two hours just to kill time, wishing I had someone or something to go home to. The old me would have wanted to fix this stressful time for Emma. I would feel guilty and apologize for having so much free time and offer to come over, clean her house, and take the kids for a month. But this wasn't my responsibility, just like it wasn't her responsibility to drop whatever she had going on to come hang out with me for the day because she knew I was lonely. Being twins, we always took on each other's struggles and triumphs. We were each other's secure and safe place throughout our lives. Because we had both done inward work and been in therapy, getting rid of that codependent behavior that was drilled into us at such a young age, we were now at a place when we had healthy communication and boundaries with one another. We honored our individual journeys, helped each other in supportive ways, and didn't compare our lives against one another. Even though it wasn't a romantic relationship, it was the most important one in my life, and I was successfully using all of the tools I had been working on and was proud of myself.

The day had come when my friends and I were no longer all single—they all were in amazing relationships except for me. I was the last single one of the group, and it made me feel a bit insecure. I was so happy for them, and I also gained three new people in my life who I adored, but I was feeling like the odd one out for the first time with my friends. My friends had always been my saving grace when it came to feeling judged by society and everyone else around me. We were all living our lives and embracing that we didn't have anything tying us down. We would go wherever we wanted, had no one to check in with, could spend our money on our own, and we were thriving. After working all week, our weekends consisted of nights out filled with great food, alcohol, tons of laughs, and meeting new people. Wherever we were, we would all end up back together in the morning at one of our apartments, ordering McDonald's breakfast while we recapped the night. At thirty, it was like I was doing what I should have been doing in my twenties. When I was twenty-four, I owned a home, was already engaged, and cooked dinner for my fiancé and myself every night. Now, here I was going out all of the time while my whole Instagram feed was filled with people buying houses and having babies. As much as I knew it was where I was supposed to be, I judged myself. I judged myself for feeling like I failed, like I was going backward in life. As time went by, and as one by one my friends started to find their partners, I found myself comparing myself to others again. I felt once again like I didn't belong, and I started feeling very alone again.

Comparison is a really toxic thought that unfortunately comes naturally to many of us. Social media does not make this any easier. The open display of living your best life and sharing the triumphs can be a positive outlet, for sure; but at that time, while I was going through a hard time, it was impossible for me to not compare my life to the IG reel. There were countless times when I was in my healing journey and would be feeling positive, happy, and like I'd come so far, but then I would open IG and see yet another couple announcing their engagement or their pregnancy. It would pull me back into the mindset of feeling behind in life, even with the happiness I would feel for the good news I was seeing. It took a lot of work for me to be able to change this mindset and dialogue with myself. Eventually, I was able to be happy for other people without internally putting myself down for being in a different place. To be honest, it made me reflect on myself and my own journey with social media. I was the girl with the new house post, the engagement post, the big wedding video, yet it all fell apart very shortly after. I didn't post: "My husband left me for another girl and I'm getting divorced" or "First night alone in my new apartment with no furniture." In fact, during this time while I was at my absolute lowest, I posted a picture of myself with a big smile on my face posing in a red phone booth in London for my "Glamorous Work Trip." I posted pictures of me looking very thin because I wanted people to think I looked "better," even though I was unhealthier than ever. People mostly post and share the good, what they want you to see, so know that these are only small snippets of what is going on in someone's life and do not warrant an opportunity for comparison or to judge yourself.

Shortly after this, my friend Stefani and her partner got engaged. They were planning their wedding in Mexico and after not traveling for over two years, I was so excited to be taking this trip with all of my best friends to celebrate such a special occasion. I was traveling with four couples, and pretty much everyone who was going to be there was coupled up. My ego immediately started the negative dialogue: *You're a loser! You're a seventh wheel! You can't find one person to go to Mexico with!*

As the thoughts flowed through my mind, I was fully aware of how ridiculous they sounded, and also how untrue they all were. No one thought any of these things about me, except for me. I changed the dialogue immediately: *How lucky am I that I had a trip to go on like this? How lucky was I that I had all of my best friends going who never once made me feel like I was tagging along? How lucky am I that I am at the point where I can afford this vacation on my own and I get to have my own room? How lucky am I that I can do whatever I want and make this trip whatever I want for myself?*

I embraced this vacation. The old me would wait to see what everyone else's plans were and would have just tagged along with that. I was fully comfortable doing things by myself. It wasn't like I woke up one day and just did this, but through the last few years of being single, and being alone, and pushing myself to do things here and there eventually turned into me being really independent, and I loved it! I learned I really am in charge of my own happiness. I could be negative and think about everything I didn't have on this trip, or I could lean into everything I did have. I was up early every morning; I would get my coffee, walk around the resort, then meditate on the beach before meeting my friends for breakfast. I booked a two-hour massage one day and did one of those creepy fish pedicures on another day. It was the perfect balance of celebrating my friends, having my alone time, and spending time with so many great people building amazing memories.

I encourage you, no matter if you are single, married, divorced, a single parent, or whatever stage of life you are in, to pay attention to times you want to do something but feel you cannot for whatever reason. Start slow, start small, and start integrating it into your life. I had a whole comfortable plan that was turned upside down one day, and I was thrown into being alone full force. I had to sit in the uncomfortableness of this and push past this fear. If someone ever told me that one day I would love being home alone, I would have told them they were absolutely nuts. But I am living proof that it is possible. Now, if I have fear surrounding something, I lean into it even more. I ask myself where is the fear coming from? What am I scared of happening? What is the worst that could happen if I just try? Five years ago, I wouldn't have even showered by myself until Tony came home because I was afraid of doing this in an empty house. What if I had just taken the shower? I would have saved a lot of time and worry that's for sure because the day did come when I had no choice and had to, and it was fine.

LET'S CHECK IN

Finding peace in where you are in life can have its ups and downs. Fighting it, however, won't help.

- Are there areas in your life where you're still comparing yourself with others?
- How can you change this today?
- Can you name three positives in your current situation?

what's working

I reflect a lot throughout my healing journey every few months on things I like about my life and on things that might need work or shifting. I check in to see what's working and what's not, and I write it all down. I acknowledge all of it and bring awareness to these areas moving forward. I try to do this monthly! For example, I'll write something like this:

What's working?
My flexible work schedule
Therapy
My work-life balance
Alcohol detox

What needs work?

Saving money

Self-confidence & body image issues

Judgment

Diet

I realize that I am living the life that I once prayed for. There was a time when I couldn't shut my brain off and couldn't sleep no matter how hard I tried. I couldn't afford to get my nails done, and I would never be caught dead sitting at a coffee shop by myself because of what I thought I'd look like to others. Now, it is something I genuinely enjoy and look forward to each week. I no longer feel the need to explain where I was at in my life. With this, I was still constantly faced with "Why haven't you met someone yet?"; "So and so just met someone online. You should try it"; "Are you going out to the right places? This is where you need to be"; and "Why am I not hearing you tell me that you hooked up with a new guy and that you're dating all the time? You need to go out more!"

These questions drove me absolutely nuts. Despite me knowing in my gut that this is where I was meant to be at that time. I felt that until I was walking down the aisle again, everyone was still going to categorize me as the damaged girl who was cheated on and left for someone else who can't find a guy. It was like I wasn't enough on my own. No one could believe that I really was feeling at peace and happier than I had been in a long time. I would run into people and the first thing they would still say is "No guy yet?"

I would have conversations telling them everything that was going on in my life, and I could see it in their eyes that they wouldn't even be listening and were waiting for me to pause and say, "And I have a date this weekend." I would be internally SCREAMING: *I live on my own! I got myself out of debt and built my credit back up! I pay my rent and all of my bills on time! I got promoted at work three times this year! I have a new car! I take my garbage out twice a week! I can put furniture together! I'm in therapy addressing real shit! I'm a rule follower! I'm always on time! I never get pulled over! I travel! I get my teeth cleaned every three months! My family and friends know they can count on me for anything! I can make a kick-ass espresso martini! Stop asking me if I met someone! Who gives a flying fuck?!*

I wasn't half of this person when I was in my marriage, yet people saw me as "fulfilled and okay" back then. Why? Because I had a husband? I know it came from a caring and loving place, especially from my family, but it was beyond frustrating. I tried the apps, I was going out, I was open to it, but it just didn't come to me as fast and as natural. I was not about to force it, and I certainly was not about to settle for anything or anyone, especially after what I had gone through.

Journal Entry—July 2022

It is another Sunday morning in July, which is once again one of my favorite days. I relaxed in bed until 11 a.m. because I was out last night with all of my friends having an amazing meal where we ordered pretty much one of everything on the menu. We had finished the night off dancing, drinking espresso martinis, and blasting Spice Girls the whole way home.

Reminiscing on the night before, I got out of bed, threw on a baseball hat and leggings and went to get my favorite overpriced coffee to drink while I went food shopping for the week at Trader Joes, then strolled through Target. I went to see Emma and my nieces and got my fix of hugs, kisses, and dance parties. I headed home and it was 80 degrees and breezy, so I sat outside for the rest of the day, writing, meditating, organizing my week, and just being present in the peaceful life I had created.

I love this life that I have built. I love my dinners for one on my couch watching Bravo. I embrace it because I know I may miss it one day. I will be showered and in bed by 8 p.m., with clean sheets, the fan on, and a new Netflix show. The fact that society looks at this life of mine as "sad" is the saddest part. I am happy, I am content, and I am at peace.

Days like that one in July make me grateful for my journey. Grateful for how far I've come, that I held out, and that I didn't settle. Grateful to have the privilege of me and my time. It doesn't have to make sense to anyone else, it doesn't have to look anything like anyone else's journey or life. It only has to make sense to you. If you do one thing and one thing only for yourself, create your own happiness and peace and know exactly what that means for you.

LET'S CHECK IN

Write a paragraph describing yourself and your life. Are you happy with it?

Take a moment with this one. It's a big question. Focus on what comes up.

always moving forward

I never had that one moment that was my "spiritual awakening." I had little moments, little triumphs through the years that led me to this moment now. It was the way I started handling certain things here and there that turned into my new normal. I started saying no and respecting the boundaries I had set for myself. I no longer accepted unacceptable behavior. I was still there for the people around me, but I prioritized myself and my mental health first.

Can I say I love myself yet? No, I cannot. I feel like I am on that path, and I will one day. Do I like myself? Yeah, I do. More than I ever have before. Do I have bad days? Absolutely! It is all a process and the journey that

I am on—that we are all on. Some days I feel so proud of how far I have come. I look back at the person I was, and I am so proud of that girl for getting out of the dark place she was in, taking the hand that was dealt to her, getting her hair out from in front of her face, being the best she could at the time, and choosing to be better. There are some days, I feel like a fraud and that goes against everything I know and that I truly believe in. Some days, I make the wrong decisions and let myself have that bad day, but I won't let myself stay there. I get centered and bounce back. I don't beat myself up for it either. I trust that every day is a part of the path that I am meant to be on. I am sure I will always be a little triggered by the smell of pumpkin candles or hearing a loud pickup truck drive by. I still cringe a little every time I pass that gym parking lot, but I know how to acknowledge the triggers now and move on from them, and sometimes, even honor them and how much progress I've made.

The day did eventually come when the pit in my stomach went away and I was able to wake up and go a day without thinking of Tony. Days turned into weeks, and even now when I think of him, it's usually honoring the good that we had and hoping he found the happiness he was looking for as well. I realize it truly was all temporary. I am not a perfect person. I won't ever claim to be at all, but I do try my best every day to stay balanced, DIG deep, check in with myself, and stay true to my authentic self. I have no idea what is next for me, but I am committed to staying grounded and having faith that everything else will continue to fall into place—and I encourage you to do the same. Every time I have questioned my faith, it always found its way back to prove me wrong, so I continue to lean into it.

Once you realize who your authentic self is, no one can take that away from you. Through this process, you'll notice that people around you may change, and that is okay. You may lose people, but you will gain people too. People who respect you for who you truly are, not what you offer them. You have the responsibility to set the tone for your life, for who you are, what you want, what you feel you deserve, and what you will and will not tolerate. This is your right and one of the first steps to creating the life you want. Focus on being the person who you want to be and surround yourself with people who bring out the best parts of you, not the worst.

Our bodies tell us when we feel off or triggered by someone, and we have to pay attention to those feelings. If you are in a situation like family dynamics or co-parenting where you cannot necessarily remove people from your life, work on setting clear boundaries with them. Check in with yourself and become very clear on where you stand to protect yourself and your emotions. Especially in these encounters. Notice if you are becoming defensive, triggered, or a version of you that you do not necessarily like and take a step back, take some deep breaths, go for a walk, listen to some music, put on a TV show that makes you laugh, and revisit the conversation or situation after you are calm and balanced.

For anyone struggling with self-worth, experiencing heartbreak, betrayal, grief, starting over, at a crossroads, or going through any type of transition in general, the one thing I can say for sure is no matter how sad or how low you may feel in this moment, it will get better, and it will get easier. *I promise.* It is the one thing I wish someone had told me back then. The experiences you have had and the pain that came along with it will never completely go away, but it will start to diminish and eventually shape you into the person you are. You will find a new normal, you will find things that bring you clarity, peace, and belly laughs that will overshadow the hurt and sadness you once felt. You will look back one day and not have the same feelings and reactions that you once had toward certain people or situations. You will realize how strong you are and how far you have come, and your story will 100 percent help others.

conclusion

It's all temporary, babe. Every tear, every heartbreak, every fear. Even the good times will come and go. The laughter, the joy, the late nights, and the early mornings. Celebrate the highs, and be kind to yourself in the lows. Every day we have is a gift, an opportunity to strengthen our relationships with ourselves, which is the most important and fulfilling one of all.

I'm right there with you as you continue experiencing the twists and turns, and you can follow me on my journey, because it's not over yet! If you loved this read, make sure to tag me as well. It feels odd to ask that, but like I've shared in my book, it was connections with people who saw me as I was, not what I had been through, that made a big difference.

An arrow can only be shot by pulling it backward. So, when life is dragging you back with difficulties, it means that it's going to launch you into something great. So just focus, and keep aiming.

–PAULO COELHO

acknowledgments

I want to thank every person who has been on this journey with me.

Krystie for coming into this wild life with me and for being by my side every single day, my other half, my true soulmate in this world.

My parents for loving and supporting me unconditionally and always encouraging me to do whatever I wanted to do. Kelly, Dennis, and Tom for all of the amazing memories growing up and for always being there.

Aunt Carol and Uncle Vinny for always treating me as if I was your own. My cousins for all the support over the last few years and the many, many laughs.

Christie, Paul, and Meghan for coming back into my life when I needed it most and for the endless memories we have created since. Dina, Anne Marie, Ashlee, Jamie, and Dana for never leaving my side and always being people I could count on, no matter the circumstances.

The YGTMedia community and Sabrina Greer for guiding me and making my dream of writing a book come true. Cassie Jeans for your constant support, wisdom, and encouragement, I couldn't have done this without you.

To the Jesses in my life who made me never feel alone, who never let me down, who helped me heal, and helped me grow.

Lastly, my littlest loves, Serena and Mila for showing me a love so great and filling my heart up in a way I never knew possible. I love you.

resources

(in alphabetical order)

Books

Gary Chapman, *The Five Love Languages: The Secret to Love That Lasts*, 1992

Deepak Chopra, *The Seven Spiritual Laws of Success*, 1994

Michael A. Singer, *The Untethered Soul: The Journey Beyond Yourself*, 2007

Websites

The American Yoga Academy, americanyogaacademy.com

GabbyBernstein.com

RisingWoman.com

YogaWithAdriene.com

YGTMedia Co. is a blended boutique publishing house for mission-driven humans. We help seasoned and emerging authors "birth their brain babies" through a supportive and collaborative approach. Specializing in narrative nonfiction and adult and children's empowerment books, we believe that words can change the world, and we intend to do so one book at a time.

 ygtmedia.co/publishing

@ygtmedia.company

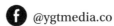 @ygtmedia.co